What is African An Literature?

Margo N. Crawford

WILEY Blackwell

This edition first published 2021
© 2021 John Wiley & Sons, Inc.

All rights reserved. No part of this publication may be reproduced, stored in a retrieval system, or transmitted, in any form or by any means, electronic, mechanical, photocopying, recording or otherwise, except as permitted by law. Advice on how to obtain permission to reuse material from this title is available at http://www.wiley.com/go/permissions.

The right of Margo N. Crawford to be identified as the author of this work and has been asserted in accordance with law.

Registered Office
John Wiley & Sons, Inc., 111 River Street, Hoboken, NJ 07030, USA

Editorial Office
111 River Street, Hoboken, NJ 07030, USA

For details of our global editorial offices, customer services, and more information about Wiley products visit us at www.wiley.com.

Wiley also publishes its books in a variety of electronic formats and by print-on-demand. Some content that appears in standard print versions of this book may not be available in other formats.

Limit of Liability/Disclaimer of Warranty
While the publisher and authors have used their best efforts in preparing this work, they make no representations or warranties with respect to the accuracy or completeness of the contents of this work and specifically disclaim all warranties, including without limitation any implied warranties of merchantability or fitness for a particular purpose. No warranty may be created or extended by sales representatives, written sales materials or promotional statements for this work. The fact that an organization, website, or product is referred to in this work as a citation and/or potential source of further information does not mean that the publisher and authors endorse the information or services the organization, website, or product may provide or recommendations it may make. This work is sold with the understanding that the publisher is not engaged in rendering professional services. The advice and strategies contained herein may not be suitable for your situation. You should consult with a specialist where appropriate. Further, readers should be aware that websites listed in this work may have changed or disappeared between when this work was written and when it is read. Neither the publisher nor authors shall be liable for any loss of profit or any other commercial damages, including but not limited to special, incidental, consequential, or other damages.

Library of Congress Cataloging-in-Publication Data
Name: Crawford, Margo N., 1969– author.
Title: What is African American literature? / by Margo N. Crawford.
Description: First edition. | Hoboken : Wiley-Blackwell, 2020. | Series: Wiley Blackwell manifestos | Includes bibliographical references and index.
Identifiers: LCCN 2020021084 (print) | LCCN 2020021085 (ebook) | ISBN 9781119123347 (paperback) | ISBN 9781119123378 (adobe pdf) | ISBN 9781119123361 (epub)
Subjects: LCSH: American literature–African American authors–History and criticism. | Affect (Psychology) in literature. | Slavery in literature. | African Americans in literature.
Classification: LCC PS153.N5 C76 2020 (print) | LCC PS153.N5 (ebook) | DDC 810.9/896073–dc23
LC record available at https://lccn.loc.gov/2020021084
LC ebook record available at https://lccn.loc.gov/2020021085

Cover Design: Wiley
Cover Image: African American woman, half-length portrait, facing left, reading book by Fæ is licensed under Creative Commons CC0

Set in 11.5/14pt Bembo by SPi Global, Pondicherry, India
Printed and bound by CPI Group (UK) Ltd, Croydon, CR0 4YY

10 9 8 7 6 5 4 3 2 1

What is African American Literature?

Wiley Blackwell Manifestos

In this series major critics make timely interventions to address important concepts and subjects, including topics as diverse as, for example: Culture, Race, Religion, History, Society, Geography, Literature, Literary Theory, Shakespeare, Cinema, and Modernism. Written accessibly and with verve and spirit, these books follow no uniform prescription but set out to engage and challenge the broadest range of readers, from undergraduates to postgraduates, university teachers, and general readers – all those, in short, interested in ongoing debates and controversies in the humanities and social sciences.

Already Published

The Idea of Culture	Terry Eagleton
The Future of Christianity	Alister E. McGrath
Reading After Theory	Valentine Cunningham
21st-Century Modernism	Marjorie Perloff
The Future of Theory	Jean-Michel Rabaté
True Religion	Graham Ward
Inventing Popular Culture	John Storey
Myths for the Masses	Hanno Hardt
The Future of War	Christopher Coker
The Rhetoric of RHETORIC	Wayne C. Booth
When Faiths Collide	Martin E. Marty
The Future of Environmental Criticism	Lawrence Buell
The Idea of Latin America	Walter D. Mignolo
The Future of Society	William Outhwaite
Provoking Democracy	Caroline Levine
Rescuing the Bible	Roland Boer
Our Victorian Education	Dinah Birch
The Idea of English Ethnicity	Robert Young
Living with Theory	Vincent B. Leitch
Uses of Literature	Rita Felski
Religion and the Human Future	David E. Klemm and William Schweiker
The State of the Novel	Dominic Head
In Defense of Reading	Daniel R. Schwarz
Why Victorian Literature Still Matters	Philip Davis
The Savage Text	Adrian Thatcher
The Myth of Popular Culture	Perry Meisel
Phenomenal Shakespeare	Bruce R. Smith
Why Politics Can't Be Freed From Religion	Ivan Strenski
What Cinema is!	Andrew Dudley
The Future of Christian Theology	David F. Ford
A Future for Criticism	Catherine Belsey
After the Fall	Richard Gray
After Globalization	Eric Cazdyn and Imre Szeman
Art Is Not What You Think It Is	Donald Preziosi and Claire Farago
The Global Future of English Studies	James F. English
The Future of Jewish Theology	Steven Kepnes
Where is American Literature?	Caroline Levander
New England Beyond Criticism	Elisa New
Philosophy and the Study of Religions	Kevin Schilbrack
The Future for Creative Writing	Graeme Harper
Breaking the Book: Print Humanities in the Digital Age	Laura Mandell

Contents

Acknowledgments	vii
Introduction: The Affective Atmosphere of African American Literature	1
1 The Textual Production of Black Affect: The Blush of Toni Morrison's Last Novel	25
2 Mood Books	55
3 The Vibrations of African American Literature	73
4 *Shiver:* The Diasporic Shock of Elsewhere	103
5 Twitch *or* Wink: The Literary *Afterlife of the Afterlife* of Slavery	135
CODA	175
Index	179

Acknowledgments

This book was greatly inspired by Cheryl Wall's groundbreaking study *Worrying the Line: Black Women Writers, Lineage, and Literary Tradition* (2005). African American literary traditions (as Cheryl Wall taught us) are a worrying of lines (lines being understood as lineage, intertextuality, improvisation, and the elasticity of blackness).

In these early years of the twenty-first century, scholars of African American literature and theory have been gathering, at a wide range of conferences and other events, to begin to theorize the emergent forms, moods, and stories that distinguish twenty-first century African American literature from earlier flows. These forums, looking at new directions in African American literature and theory, propelled the questions explored in this book's reshaping of the title of Kenneth W. Warren's *What Was African American Literature?* (2011) into the question of what it *is* (on the lower frequencies).

So many scholars make me hear these lower frequencies of black aesthetics. I thank Cheryl Wall, Eleanor Traylor, Hortense Spillers, Haki Madhubuti, Houston A. Baker, Dana Williams, Kokahvah Zauditu-Selassie, Fred Moten, Farah Jasmine Griffin, Kevin Quashie, Candice Jenkins, Alexis Pauline Gumbs, Soyica Colbert, Brent Edwards, Erica Edwards, Evie Shockley, L.H. Stallings, Jennifer DeVere Brody, Stephen Best, Yogita Goyal, Aida Levy-Hussen, Carter Mathes, Badia Ahad, Howard Rambsy, Meta DuEwa Jones, Greg Thomas, Lawrence Jackson, Koritha Mitchell,

Acknowledgments

Aldon Lynn Nielsen, Dagmawi Woubshet, Sharon Holland, Douglas Jones, Robert Reid Pharr, Mark Anthony Neal, George Hutchinson, and many more. I thank Richard Samson for his consummate work as editor. I thank the anonymous readers for their great insight.

Introduction: The Affective Atmosphere of African American Literature

STEPHEN COLBERT: "You have said you don't necessarily like to be pigeonholed as an African American writer. What would you like me to pigeonhole you as? (Audience laughs) Because I have to categorize everybody. […] How should I just see you as a category? If you don't want to *be* an African American writer, how should I *think* of you?" (italics mine)

TONI MORRISON: "As an American writer." (Audience cheers) (2014)

When Toni Morrison insists, in a 1993 interview, that African American literature "pulls from something that's closer to the edge," she makes the idea of African American literature sound more like an energy force than an enterprise, marketing structure, or stable, mappable tradition.[1] Morrison's emphasis, in this same interview, on the "more human future" of the idea of African American literature,

---

What is African American Literature?, First Edition. Margo N. Crawford.
© 2021 John Wiley & Sons, Inc. Published 2021 by John Wiley & Sons, Inc.

What is African American Literature?

clearly underscores the constant rewriting of what it means to be human in African American literature, but Morrison also gestures toward the idea of African American literature as that which is both "here" and "not yet here." The interview unfolds as follows:

MORRISON: I would like to write novels that were unmistakably mine, but nevertheless fit first into African American traditions and second of all, this whole thing called literature.
INTERVIEWER: First African American?
MORRISON: Yes.
INTERVIEWER: ... rather than the whole of literature?
MORRISON: Oh yes.
INTERVIEWER: Why?
MORRISON: It's richer. It has more complex sources. It pulls from something that's closer to the edge, it's much more modern. It has a human future. (1993)

For Morrison, what is modern about the idea of African American literature is its evocation of "a more human future." Alain Locke, one of the prime theorists of black modernism, offers one way to understand Morrison's gesture to the black modernist "more human future." In 1925, as Locke thinks about the style of the young New Negro Movement poets, he muses, "Our poets have stopped speaking for the Negro—they speak as Negroes. Where formerly they spoke to others and tried to interpret, they now speak to their own and try to express. They have stopped posing, being nearer the attainment of poise."[2] The difference between "pose" and "poise" is the difference between a state of identity, overdetermined by an external gaze, and a state of self-possession (even if that possession is what Fred Moten describes as being possessed by dispossession).[3] When Morrison, in the 1993 interview, insists that the idea of African American literature is *edge* work and profoundly modern, she gestures toward what Locke describes as

2

Introduction: The Affective Atmosphere of African American Literature

the black modernist, New Negro art of no longer speaking to others and trying to interpret. For Locke, the *is-ness* of African American literature emerges when writers stop "speaking for" black people and "speak as" black people (when they "stop posing" and approach the "attainment of poise").[4]

Are there formal lines (or wavy lines that seem more like vibrations) that separate African American literature that "speaks as black" and American literature at large? Is there anything distinctive about black literature that allows us to know *this is what makes it black*? Is the only distinctive feature the fact that the authors are black?

African American literature is a strategic abstraction. When literary scholars were convinced that *Incidents in the Life of a Slave Girl* was written by a white abolitionist, it was not framed as a foundational text in a tradition of African American literature. Now, its tropes are routinely used to help define a tradition. In the late 1980s, when it was established that *Incidents* was written by Harriet Jacobs, the book became a centerpiece in the architecture of African American literature. Proving the black authorship (and reading Harriet Jacobs' letters that emphasize her desire to "give …[my story] from my own hand") made it possible to read this slave narrative as a literal expression of the black desire to break out of white-dominated space, and an expression of a desire for a black interior (and not only a desire for a literary transaction across a color line).[5] It is easy to critique the equation of black identity and black book, but what if we let go of the very impulse to critique the limits of the equation of the blackness of the author and the blackness of the text, and lean into the *is-ness* produced by the texts that, for better or worse, have been marked as "African American"?

When Walter Benn Michaels expresses frustration with the emphasis on feeling in reader response interpretations of literature, he unintentionally expresses the inexhaustible possibilities of "is-ness" that animate this book's "reading for feeling" approach. Michaels asserts, "it [literature] is made literally uninterpretable but also literally inexhaustible since how it is perceived—not only what it looks like but what it makes you feel like, what it makes you think of—must be a function not only of what it is but of who you are."[6] In *What is African American Literature?*, I am letting the "what it is" bleed into "who we are" (we people whose "quiet walk down the street," as Gwendolyn Brooks mused, "is a speech to the people. Is a rebuke, is a plea, is a school").[7] I am re-hearing Fred Moten's words in *In The Break*: "What is needed is an improvisation of the transition from descent to cut [...]" (70). The line of descent (the genealogy of an is-ness of African American literature) is a cut-up formation, a *cut-up blackness* (blackness felt and lived by cut-up people). The idea of the "transition from descent to cut" helps me arrive at an understanding of how the history of the African American literary tradition is *cut up* when we focus on the black feeling (readers' and authors') that produces whatever African American literature is (outside of historical determinism and inside black improvisation). Ralph Ellison's famous musing, in *Invisible Man*, on what it means to be "outside of history" offers a way of understanding the unmappable nature of the is-ness of African American literature.[8] Just as Ellison's unnamed narrator meditates on what it means to be "outside of history" as he stares at young men wearing oversized zoot suits as they wait on a subway platform for the train to arrive, I see the is-ness of African American literature as the feeling of black excess (as the aesthetic edge that cannot be historicized because the is-ness is what is felt as one waits on the platform and is pulled into the zoot suit). Ellison's Invisible Man asks himself, "What if history was a gambler, instead of a force in a laboratory experiment [...]?" (441). This question is reshaped when we imagine what African American literature is outside of its reduction to the cultural production of black people needing to write ourselves into a history that erased us. Echoing the Invisible Man's question about the zoot-suiters, on the subway platform, who are "running and dodging the forces of history" (441), the question becomes, "What if African American literature is a gambler, instead of a force in a laboratory experiment?" The black affective atmosphere (what really distinguishes African American literature) is not felt when one gets on the train of historical determinist approaches to African American literature.

Introduction: The Affective Atmosphere of African American Literature

My emphasis on what is *felt* can make us rethink Robert Stepto's dismissal of feeling (as a way of interpreting African American literature) during the late 1970s black literary theory attempt to break out of sociological and "non-literary" approaches to teaching African American literature.[9] In a key passage in *Afro-American Literature: The Reconstruction of Instruction* (1978), Stepto makes the turn to "feeling" seem like the stale approaches to the literature that crush the art and make all study of African American literature a historical or sociological study of African Americans. He writes:

> Those students who, as Ralph Ellison reports, persist in the illusion that they possess a 'genetic' knowledge of black culture, may very well compose yet another all-purpose 'black' essay. Others will take the harder but more rewarding path delineated—and in fact demanded—by the multiple forms of literacy, not "feeling," and draw from *all* their resources the requisite vision and energy to see author, text, and tradition alike. (15)

But the role of feeling in the *is-ness* of African American literature can be a deep refusal of the impulse to reduce the art to history and sociology. Feeling is what matters most when we wonder what African American literature *is* within what Raymond Williams calls a "sociology of culture," a "sociology of a new kind," that makes room for culture as a "structure of feeling."[10]

The *is-ness* of African American literature is also a feeling of the present. In *What is the Present?*, Michael North wonders, "Does it make sense to think of the present as radically distinct from the time around it, from which it seems to emerge and into which it seems to blend?" The present "is-ness" (the "new" and "contemporary") of African American literature has been a recursive conversation. The contemporary (as proclaimed, in 1970s vernacular, as "what it is, what it is") is, of course, restaged constantly. The New Negro movement of the 1920s and 1930s announced this newness in such an emphatic manner, the words "new breed" were mobilized during the 1960s and 70s Black Arts movement, and Trey Ellis' 1989 essay "The New Black Aesthetic" anticipates all of the "newness" dramatized in twenty-first century frames of the "new black." The contemporary (the newness) is constantly evoked, throughout the twentieth and twenty-first century, as black writing continues to be a way that people feel less shackled by "what was."

Like Michael Gillespie's approach to the "idea" of black film, I frame my questions around the "idea" of African American literature, as opposed to an approach that aims to identify texts that are in or outside the "fact" of African American literature.[11] The idea of African American literature is different from the "structure" of African American literature (that which Henry Louis Gates, in such a generative fashion, uncovered in *The Signifying Monkey* in 1987 as the field of African American literary criticism was set in motion). Gates brilliantly studies intertextuality in order to unveil the structure of African American literature. I focus on affect (the blush, the shiver, the vibration, and the twitch and wink) in order to unveil the limits of historicizing approaches to the "idea" of African American literature. African American literature is an archive of feelings, the tradition of a tension between individual affect and historical structure. As Alexis Pauline Gumbs writes, "Breathing seems individual but it is also so profoundly collective."[12] I approach the collectivity of African American literature as acts of breathing in charged air. The notion of charged air opens up a new dimension of literary tradition, a sense that "tradition" could be re-felt as the sensuous, atmospheric experience of texts. At this late date in the unfolding of African American literary studies, we need more room for an understanding of African American literary flows as the circulation of affective energy against and within the structures of history. Whatever the shared flow is, it is a flow of feeling created as books are read alongside each other (what John Akomfrah calls an "affective proximity").[13]

Amiri Baraka conveys the idea of tradition as atmosphere when he begins his 2005 poetry volume *The Book of Monk* with an epigraph that includes the words "*the air running in and out of you.*" The practice of African American literature often makes the shared atmosphere of affect matter as much as the themes of black life that are often viewed as the private property of African American literature. Lauren Berlant, in *Cruel Optimism* (2011), foregrounds the "shared atmosphere" of affect. She writes, "[A]ffective atmospheres are shared, not solitary, and [...] bodies are continuously busy judging their environments and responding to the atmospheres in which they find themselves" (15). Approaching African American literature as an affective atmosphere changes the women studies' paradigm of "writing on the body." When we think of African American literature as a shared atmosphere, we arrive at "writing with the body." In the essay "Souls Grown Deep" (2006), in which Amiri Baraka directly focuses on the "is-ness" of African American literature, when he refers to the "creative is ness of what are" (*Razor*, 394), he describes writing with the body through formulations such as the "poet is an organ of registered flesh" and "a real cry from a real person." And, in "Technology and Ethos," Baraka makes writing with the body gain full shape when he imagines the "expression-scriber" (alternative typewriter) that involves the entire body, not only fingertips. He writes:

> A typewriter?—why shd it only make use of the tips of the fingers as contact points of flowing multi directional creativity. If I invented a word placing machine, an 'expression-scriber', *if you will*, then I would have a kind of instrument into which I could step & sit or sprawl or hang & use not only my fingers to make words express feelings but elbows, feet, head, behind, and all the sounds I wanted, screams, grunts, taps, itches [...][14]

In *M Archive: After the End of the World*, Alexis Pauline Gumbs imagines that fingertips can do what Baraka needs the entire body to do. She writes, "they attended to their fingertips" (51). As Gumbs describes the intensity of the "pulsing fingers" and "muscle memory" (and the "channeling" of memory "into hands"), she, like Baraka, foregrounds the process of writing with the body.[15] The body of black literature is produced by the tension of the flesh that has been named the "black body." The tension is the "open system of nervousness" of African American literature.[16] As Ashon T. Crawley theorizes about the breath of black aesthetics, he presents this idea of the "open system of nervousness," and leans on Susan Buck-Morss' insistence that "the nervous system is not contained within the body's limits" (Crawley 52-53). An open system of black nervousness (an open system of black feeling) distinguishes African American literature from other literary traditions.

Jean Toomer links the words "emotion" and "Negro" in a letter, written in 1922, to Waldo Frank. Toomer states, "The only time that I think 'Negro' is when I want a peculiar emotion which is associated with this name" (131, *Modernism and Affect*). We can easily read this confession as Toomer's internalization of a racialized primitivist notion of black passion, but this confession might also push us to re-read Toomer's *Cane* as a classic example of how the practice of African American literature often becomes the practice of working narrative for its most affective possibilities. When we read *Cane* through this lens of affect, the opening image "Her skin is like dusk / on the eastern horizon/ O cant you see it" is a striking image of *black blush*. The most striking image of affect as uncontained intensity and as a way of understanding the interaction between the personal and the impersonal may be the opening words in Toomer's "Fern": "Face flowed in her eyes." The loss of the definite article signals that this aesthetic flow is the transmission of affect, not the transmission of the "definite article" of literary historicism that disciplines affect (that makes an archive of feelings become an archive of who is definitively within or outside "African American literature").

Alice Walker, in *In Search of Our Mother's Gardens* (1983), advises that "we" (those of us who are invested in the ongoing tradition of black aesthetics) keep *Cane* and let Toomer go.[17] But how could we ever hold the aesthetic of evanescence that shapes the opening affect-laden portraits in *Cane*? Fred Moten, in *The Feel Trio*, writes, "Cutting around corners puts me in mind of jean toomer, I think I'll change my name to gene tumor. I want to be a stream tuner, unfurled in tongues that won't belong in anybody's mouth, mass swerving from the law of tongues." The practice of cutting pivots

Introduction: The Affective Atmosphere of African American Literature

on an alternative kinship that can hurt and make one feel like "gene tumor," or make one feel like a "stream tuner," a creator of streams of feeling. As Brian Massumi explains, "[F]eelings have a way of folding into each other, resonating together, interfering with each other, mutually intensifying, all in unquantifiable ways" (1). In *What is African American Literature*, I'm cutting around corners and feeling this flow of feelings that creates a literary tradition built on disruption, surprise, and contingency.

Gérard Genette writes, "More than a boundary or a sealed border, the paratext is, rather, a threshold" (*Paratexts*, 1–2). The idea of African American literature is the idea of entering into a *black book*. These words "black book" are used during the 1960s and 70s Black Arts Movement (BAM) as a way of thinking about the textual production of an entrance into a black interior. After the BAM production of black books, the idea of African American literature remains a generative surface, *a frame that remains a frame*, not a threshold *into* an understanding of interiority that is the antithesis of surface. The practice of sharing a critical edge makes literary tradition become less of an historical entity and more of an unmappable conversation, what Felice Blake refers to (*in Black Love, Black Hate: Intimate Antagonisms in African American Literature*) as the town hall meeting of African American literature (the town meeting that cannot meet anywhere else). African American literature is the performance of the shared black *edge* of a conversation.

In *Worrying the Line: Black Women Writers, Lineage, and Literary Tradition* (2005), Cheryl Wall thinks of literary tradition as a line that is *worried*. She writes, "In using the line as a metaphor for 'literary tradition,' I do not intend to imply a strictly linear progression. A worried line is not a straight line" (13). A shared edge is a way of thinking about the crooked lines, in the twenty-first century, that are making the word "tradition" become what Dionne Brand, in the novel *In Another Place, Not Here*, calls "not rip enough." The *ripped up* textual conditions of possibility is what some writers are discovering now as they make us feel what Tracy Smith, in *Life on Mars*, sees as the edges that are too linked to feel like edges as opposed to curves. Smith, in the poem "Sci-Fi," hails an art that has "no edges, but curves" (7). A curve-like edge is a way of understanding the precarious, shared edge produced by the twenty-first century *beyond the black book* impulse, embodied in texts such as Percival Everett's turn-of-the-century novel *Erasure* and Claudia Rankine's shiny, white book *Citizen*.

The Idea of the Black Book

Citizen: An American Lyric (2014) may be the signature twenty-first century text that has re-energized the inseparability of the *idea* of American literature and the *idea* of African American literature. The shiny white cover and the shiny white and thick pages in *Citizen* literally perform the shift from the BAM idea of the black book to the twenty-first century idea of the white book that can break out of a color line logic of African American literature.

The white blank pages throughout *Citizen* make the white paratext and the white interior blend as the feeling of black words on white pages and the feeling of the absence of any black words on white pages make readers experience the everyday life of race as the tension between the constant reproduction of the color line and the constant pauses when the color line is disrupted.

The blank white pages become the pause when words do not only disappear; the narrative of whiteness also disappears as we feel whiteness as a color. The tint of this whiteness is so bright it overwhelms. Rankine creates the tension between whiteness as a racial identity and whiteness as a color that does not need to feel like an oppressive force, a dominant cultural force that erases the possibility of the black book. *Citizen* might be the textual production of a color line performance that makes the idea of a radical white book become the idea of a radical black book. Rankine's inclusion of Glenn Ligon's text paintings allows the texture of the radical black book to be felt in the midst of the shiny white pages. Ligon's text paintings give words texture and make readers/viewers experience

Introduction: The Affective Atmosphere of African American Literature

surface as depth. The depth of the surface of the shiny white pages, like the depth of the black pages with Ligon's text paintings, is the surface depth that does not need the imagined interiority of a book. *Citizen* then becomes a textual production of a book that has no inner space, no post-paratext structure that we could call a narrative on race and class in America in the twenty-first century. *Citizen*'s fragmented form is a constant *gesture* to this narrative "on race and class in America in the twenty-first century." But Rankine never allows the gestures to settle into a master narrative.

Why would African American writers, creating the new territory of twenty-first century African American literature, want to write books that are multi-edged, surface oriented, with no imagined interiority? Could it be that there is a desire to imagine community in formation as opposed to community as already formed? Could the depth of surface be the depth of the surface that the process of "in formation" becomes? Before any settling, the surface is where the tensions of potential community *tingle*. In *Citizen*, when the black words "Come on. Let it go. Move on" appear on the shiny white page, we may feel the tension between remaining stuck to a surface or feeling that there is a way to move on even as we remain stuck to that surface. Re-reading these words, in *Citizen*, through the lens of this focus on the *tex*ture of the white pages, allows us to see how *Citizen* is the textual performance of a twenty-first century unmarking of the black book.

In Percival Everett's *Erasure* (2001), we see the performance of a novel within a novel and then the move to a third title page that is just an alternative title, not a novel within a novel within a novel. The third title page can easily be read as a surface that has no depth. The title "Fuck" signals Everett's exhaustion with the entire publishing industry that makes the black book mean "black representational space."[18] Throughout the novel, Everett sets up a tension between the practice of representation and the practice of abstraction. Black representational space bores the character Thelonious Ellison, also known as "Monk." Everett makes Richard Wright's 1940 novel *Native Son* signal the type of black representational space that Monk sees as defining the idea of African American literature. *My Pafology* (the novel within the novel) is a satire of *Native Son*. Everett's satire of *Native Son* is written in eye dialect. As readers sound out the unconventional spellings, the eye dialect seems as surface as the stereotypes that make black life seem like ongoing tragedy and pathology.

When we remember the impetus of Wright's autobiography *Black Boy* (1945), we gain a new way of understanding Everett's satirizing of *Native Son*, this textual *re*production of *Native Son*. Wright was inspired to write Black Boy after feeling the tension of the color line as he gave a talk to an interracial audience, in 1942, at Fisk University. Wright remembered that tension in the following manner:

> There was but little applause. Indeed, the audience was terribly still, and it was not until I was half-way through my speech that it crashed upon me that I was saying things that Negroes were not supposed to say publicly, things that whites had forbidden. What made me realize this was a hysterical, half-repressed, tense kind of laughter that *went up now and then from the white and black faces*.[19]

Everett is frustrated with Wright's production of African American literature. He moves to the production of a "tense kind of laughter" that would make Wright's books *Black Boy* and *Native Son* lose their ability to frame black life for non-black audiences. Everett's reproduction of *Native Son* aims to recapture the tension that Wright was never attempting to destroy. With the overwhelming success of *Black Boy*, Wright made interracial audiences more comfortable hearing "things that Negroes were not supposed to say publicly." Everett, in *Erasure,* is aiming to express "publicly" his frustration with what has happened between 1940 and now. Everett worries that the industry of African American literature has created a narrative that greatly limits what can be legible within black representational space.

Erasure, a deeply satirical novel, produces a laughter that might be similar to Wright's description of the tension in the lecture room at Fisk University. Everett aims to disrupt the disturbing comfort that people might have when they read about the tragedy of black lives. Everett, in *Erasure*, searches for a way to dislodge the

Introduction: The Affective Atmosphere of African American Literature

naturalized frames that made *Native Son* and *Black Boy* be read so widely and with so much acclaim. Through his use of experimental paratexts, Everett leads us to the question, can blackness be made into a critical edge of an aesthetic flow, not the critical center of an aesthetic flow? The play with paratext, in *Erasure*, becomes a play with the inside and outside of a text. Since the third title page, the title page with the word "Fuck," has no text following it that is supposed to be the inside of "Fuck," the pages before and after this floating title page dramatize the sense that this book is floating, unable to be read as a book in the way that we read a book like *Native Son*. We may read *Erasure* as Everett's desire to unhinge African American literature. Genette describes the paratext as a threshold, and Everett uses paratext to produce the sense that we remain on the edge, as opposed to entering into a book.

The 1960s and 70s Black Arts Movement was the first cultural movement that directly staged the production of books written for ideal black readers. The meaning of African American literature, during the BAM, was black interior space. The textual production of this black textual inner space also led to the movement's textual production and dramatization of the edge, the threshold between inner and outer space. This cultural movement worked surface for its deepest possibilities in a manner that was similar to the movement's insistence on the substance of style. The BAM remains the first African American cultural movement that performed the production of books written specifically for black people. In order to gain a fuller grasp of the role of textual production in the creation of the specific literary traditions that are understood as "African American," we must appreciate the BAM's explicit framing of the book as "Black." Even the color of the cover of Black Arts literary texts was often black. The founding of black-owned publishing houses was a vital part of this production of the black book. Dudley Randall founded Broadside Press in 1965, when he created a broadside of his poem "Ballad of Birmingham" that responded to the 1963 church bombing that killed four young African American girls. Third World Press (which remains the largest independent

What is African American Literature?

black press) began in Chicago in 1967, when Haki Madhubuti, Carolyn Rodgers, and Johari Amini created the first publication with a used mimeograph machine.

How did the BAM understand the idea of the black book? The black books, produced by the BAM, were the textual performance of the anti-text, the performance of writing and producing books that would be too action-oriented to be held as a precious object of highbrow capital. During the BAM, "Black" is bound as the unbound. The Black Arts impulse to make art that defied the dominant norms was tied to the impulse to make art that was too excessive to be contained in books. The dreams of artists to find more room to breathe within oppressive structures made them yearn to break out of the rules that defined painting, murals, sculpture, poetry, drama, and prose.

The movement imagined the black book as a black public space where ideal black readers meet.[20] One of the movement's most dramatic examples of the hailing of ideal black readers was the textual production of Amiri Baraka and Fundi (Billy Abernathy)'s *In Our Terribleness* (1970). The book begins with a full-page mirror image that demands that readers see their face, and the title "In Our Terribleness" inscribed on the face, as readers enter this "long image story in motion." As Baraka's words interact with Fundi's photographs, there are "spirals" of words becoming more concretely visual and photographs gaining more abstract dimensions. The text itself becomes the idea of the black book, bursting at its seams, trying to simultaneously create a sense of black embodiment and a release of blackness from any single frame.

A literal "Black Book" was published, in 1974 (one of Toni Morrison's productions while she was an editor at Random House). It matters that *The Black Book* is published as the Black Arts Movement is ending; the Black Arts Movement created space for the idea of the black book. *The Black Book* is a collection of words and images that explain the historical trauma and the cultural production of African Americans. Henry Louis Gates, Jr., has aptly referred to it as the "the ultimate treasure chest of the black experience."[21] What matters most

Introduction: The Affective Atmosphere of African American Literature

about *The Black Book* is the framing of a specifically black book as a book that contains an archive, that creates that "treasure chest" effect described by Gates. *The Black Book* is a surreal collection of slave auction ads, folklore, music lyrics, photographs, minstrelsy posters, a huge range of newspaper stories, color photographs of quilts and other examples of art created by enslaved Africans, and many other texts and images. In the preface to *The Black Book* (the original preface that also appears in the 2009 new edition, Toni Morrison begins with the words "I am The Black Book" and ends with the words "I am not complete here; there is much more,/ but there is no more time and no more space… and I have journeys to take,/ ships to name, and crews."[22] With these last words, Morrison channels the words of the slain Black Arts movement poet Henry Dumas. Six years after his murder (by a white police officer), Morrison makes his poetic words the beginning and the end of *The Black Book*. His words are not only the last words in the preface; they are also the final words framing (on the last page of the book) an untitled, undated photograph of an elderly African American man, wearing a tattered suit, sitting on a porch chair, and looking at the camera's lens with an expression that is difficult to read. Is it contempt, expectancy, or simply unknowable? The unreadability of this facial expression performs the lack of closure of *The Black Book*. Morrison's prefatory words linger, "I am not complete here." The Black Arts movement "Black Book" also has this lack of closure. Consider the final words in *In Our Terribleness:* "Now get up and go."[23]

How Do You Bind Nerve Endings?

In *In Our Terribleness*, Baraka troubles the framing devices of slave narratives, that include the signature of the former slave certifying that she or he has written the text. Given the illegality of black literacy during slavery, the powerful mission of the slave narratives is the force of people literally writing themselves into a legal existence. At one moment of pause in *In Our Terribleness*, Baraka signs his name. The signature, as Derrida argues in "Signature, Event, and Context," testifies to the presentness of the text but also the past.[24] The signature may cling to the past anterior in a way that all of the other words in *In Our Terribleness* cannot. Before the signature, Baraka writes, "And now the contact is broken," as he performs the role of the hypnotist who is leading black people to the discovery of the black gaze, black aesthetics, and a black world. When the signature appears, the "contact is broken" and the state of ecstatic trance breaks. Baraka searches for a counter-literacy that cannot be rendered legitimate by a signature of the author. He places the signature in the middle of the book, not on the first page. When we consider Baraka's signature as a riff on the framing of slave narratives, the frames "written by himself" and "written by herself," in the paratext of slave narratives, are dislodged as if it is no longer possible to know how to separate the content of African American literature from the frames that create the content. This *signature* pause (a moment of textual suspension and dramatizing of the tension between handwriting and typing) is felt most acutely when one reads the typed manuscript pages of *In Our Terribleness* in the Moorland-Spingarn collection of Baraka's papers (at Howard University). One reads the handwritten signature differently from the typed words. The reading of the signature *feels* different from the reading of the typed words in the rest of the manuscript.

The German physiologist Johannes Müller described nerve energies in the following manner: "sensation is not the conveyance to consciousness of a quality or state of an external object but rather the conveyance to consciousness of a quality or state of our nerves, brought by an external cause."[25] *In Our Terribleness* is a deeply experimental word-and-image text that calls attention to sensation as a way of understanding nerve energies without letting external objects and causes get in the way. Baraka shapes this entire book around the tension between ideology and nerve energies. In Althusser's "Ideology and Ideological State Apparatuses" (1969), the tension between ideology and the hailing of individuals as subjects emerges from the *simultaneity* of the "existence of the ideology" and the "hailing or interpellation of individuals as subjects."

Introduction: The Affective Atmosphere of African American Literature

Althusser insists, "But in reality these things happen without any succession. The existence of ideology and the hailing or interpellation of individuals as subjects are one and the same thing." In *In Our Terribleness*, Baraka performs this simultaneity of the ideology that already exists and the process of hailing that which does not exist yet. And as he and Abernathy make the entire book a sensorium, the hailing of blackness becomes the hailing of a black collective nervous system that is constantly on the verge of solidifying into the ideology that exists alongside the nerve endings of a black radicalism that is too open to serve the pedagogical functions of ideology.

The mirror on the first page of this book is the first performance of this tension between the solidity of ideology and the openness of black radical style. The mirror has the words "In Our Terribleness" engraved in the center. Readers enter into this text by looking at a reflection of their face and the words "IN OUR TERRIBLENESS" projected *on* their face (or *in* their face). A black mirror stage is performed. The words "IN OUR TERRIBLENESS," in their engraved form in this opening mirror page, have a texture that creates the feeling of words being projected *into* skin or *onto* skin. This tension between *writing on skin* and *words that touch and press against the skin* is the tension between the ideology that is written, solid, and known and sensation that can only be experienced in an ephemeral, evanescent manner. Baraka and Abernathy sustain this tension between black nationalism and black evanescence throughout the sensorium of this wondrously open book that is nevertheless given the subtitle of sheer pedagogy – "Some elements and meaning in black style." *In Our Terribleness* ultimately teaches us how to feel the sensations (the nerve endings) that always existed with and alongside all of the impulses, in 1960s and 70s black nationalism, to collect and frame "black study" as an object.

In order to feel the difference between the nerve endings in African American literature and other literary traditions, we might lean into the difference between the depiction of the "black book"

What is African American Literature?

in Bernard Malamud's *The Tenants* (1971) and *In Our Terribleness*. Malamud, in *The Tenants*, depicts two struggling writers (one white and one black) living in an abandoned building in New York City in the 1960s. Their initial friendship is torn apart by their battle to control the space of their creativity. The tension they feel in their shared, abandoned building is, ultimately, the tension between a literary aesthetic that claims a universalism and a literary aesthetic that announces its blackness. As Malamud approaches and then shatters the notion of a negotiated universalism (as they move from friendship to hating one another), the novel becomes a direct focus on the textual production of whiteness alongside the textual production of blackness. The characters, Harry Lesser and Willie Spearmint, type in their separate zones in the abandoned building

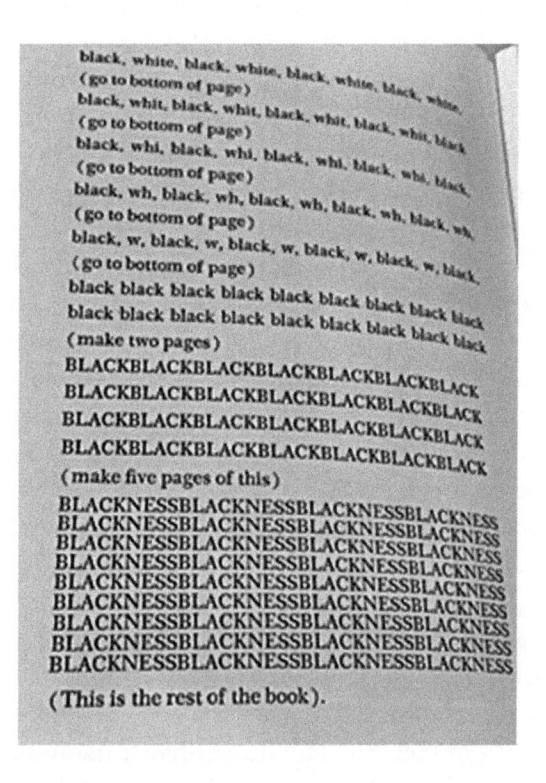

Figure 1. Bernard Malamud, *The Tenants* (1971)

Introduction: The Affective Atmosphere of African American Literature

and one of the texts, written by Willie, becomes Malamud's parody of the aesthetic warfare that shaped the Black Arts Movement. Malamud's re-production of the experimental, performative texts that shaped the BAM can be read as a satire of BAM texts that aim to create distinctive black aesthetic space through the sheer constant repetition of the words "black" and "blackness." But *The Tenants* becomes more than a dismissal of the BAM when we recognize that Malamud, consciously or unconsciously, captures the BAM impulse to create layers and depth out of repetitions that appear to be a superficial naming process. Malamud, at an earlier point in the novel, before the appearance of "Manifested Destiny," includes a scene in which Lesser (the white writer whose point of view shapes the full novel) sees Willie "sitting naked at his table, his head bent over his manuscript" (166). Lesser thinks, "Maybe he compares his flesh to his black creation on paper? Or is he mysteriously asserting the power of his blackness?" (166). Malamud's character is ridiculing the BAM-inspired writer's impulse to put black flesh on black paper and write a black world into existence, but this flesh/text tension profoundly shapes the is-ness of African American literature.

The two writers in *The Tenants* meet in an abandoned building. Lesser is a white writer who is a legal dweller and Willie is a squatter and intruder. Malamud makes Willie's creative writing sound like the endless reproduction of 1960s and 70s Black Power rhetoric, but Lesser (the white, proper tenant) is depicted as the more visionary artist who makes the abandoned building become his space of literary abandonment. The idea of African American literature is the escape from the buildings, the structures, that crush black abandonment. In the space of abandonment, black writers continue to create more space for black abandonment. The stranded embodiedness of the literature is the most distinctive feature of the body of literature. As I explore the role of affect (such as blush, vibration, shiver, twitch, and wink) in the textual production of the black book, I argue that the is-ness of African American literature is a collective nervous system. Each chapter, in this book, pivots on the affective exchanges that emerge as the idea of the black body shapes the idea of the black book. In the first chapter, Toni Morrison's critique, in her last novel, of the idea of the always already marked black body sheds light on late-style Morrison's refusal of any impulse to make African American literature a *body* of trauma. Morrison, in *God Help the Child,* her last novel published while she was alive, makes us blush as we feel a rechanneling of the final words in *Jazz*: "Look where your hands are. Now" (229). In chapter two, I uncover the role of "mood books" in the production of the idea of African American literature. Chapter three approaches the is-ness of African American literature through "vibration." I argue that poetic vibrations push against the narratives that attempt to define African American literature. In chapter four, I argue that the body of African American literature has been touched by a diasporic flow of shivers that are frozen when we continue to naturalize either the "Americanness" of the literature or the non-Americanness of the literature. I propose that the is-ness of African American literature is stranded in a space of diasporic shivers. In the final chapter, the idea of African American literature's eternal performance of the psychic hold of slavery is troubled by my focus on the difference between writers twitching from the hold of slavery and writers winking at the assumption that the theme of African American literature is, when it is all said and done (on the lowest frequencies), some version of the afterlife of slavery.

The is-ness of twenty-first century African American literature includes the current practice of the unmarking of blackness as writers become similar to Sethe's mother, in Morrison's *Beloved,* who refuses to pass on the marking of pain:

> She picked me up and carried me behind the smokehouse. Back there she opened up her dress front and lifted her breast and pointed under it. Right on her rib was a circle and a cross burnt right in the skin. She said, "This is your ma'am. This," and she pointed. "I am the only one got this mark now. The rest dead. If something happens to me and you can't tell me by my face, you can know me by this mark."

Introduction: The Affective Atmosphere of African American Literature

> Scared me so. All I could think of was how important this was and how I needed to have something important to say back, but I couldn't think of anything so I just said what I thought. "Yes, Ma'am," I said. "But how will you know me? How will you know me? Mark me, too," I said. "Mark the mark on me too." Sethe chuckled.
> "Did she?" asked Denver.
> "She slapped my face."[26]

The move to *is-ness* in contemporary African American literature is the refusal to continue the "marking of the mark." The is-ness is the trembling reading experience that is not always already marked by the black past; the is-ness is the reverberation of the slaps (the sensory shocks) that new literary spaces of black feeling are creating.

Amiri Baraka delivers one of the most direct theories of "black feeling" as the core of African American literature. In *We Are Our Feeling* (1969), Baraka's language becomes deeply experimental as he searches for the grammar that allows feeling to be the "is" of the black aesthetic. He begins this essay with a breaking down of the word "aesthetic" into "a theory in the ether" and then moves to a focus on black feeling as the alternative to the "theory in the ether." As he struggles to show that feeling, an emotional experience, is the only way to answer his opening question "What does aesthetic mean?", he finds the word "is" as he breaks out of standard English and hails the emergence of a literary tradition that will feel black. He writes:

> We are our feeling. We are our feelings ourselves. Our selves are our feelings.
> Not a theory in the ether. But feelings are central and genuine and descriptive. Life's supremest resolution is based on wisdom and love.
> How is a description of Who. So a way of feeling or the description of the process of *is* what an aesthetic wd be, (italics mine)[27]

Kenneth Warren, in *What was African American Literature?*, frames the was-ness of African American literature through the idea of the "historical entity" (8). Warren writes, "[. . .] African American literature might be viewed as a 'historical' entity rather than as the ongoing expression of a distinct people" (8). As a historical entity, African American literature would be mappable. We could determine when it begins and which writers are in the tradition, on the edge, and outside the tradition. But the mood of African American literature might show the limits of historicism. How can historicism explain black affect? Could it be that certain books feel black? What is this feeling? Is African American literature a "great realist project" that (in the full spirit of Fredric Jameson's theory of realism in *The Antinomies of Realism*) is constantly "reinforced" and "imperiled" by the evanescence of affect? Jameson argues that affect "appropriates a whole narrative apparatus and colonizes it."[28] The "whole narrative apparatus" of African American literature has always gained its strange wholeness through the uncontainable vibrations of black affect. In "Reading for Mood," Jonathan Flatley approaches mood as a "collective affective atmosphere." He writes, "Mood is a concept that gives us a way to describe the *feeling world* of these readers, if we understand mood to name a collective affective atmosphere, one structured and shaped by social forces and institutions and particular to a given historical moment" (italics mine).[29] African American literature is best understood as writers' and readers' co-creation of a black mood, of a black *feeling world*.

Notes

1 Philip Gourevitch, ed. *The Paris Review Interviews, Vol. 2*, (New York: Picador, 2007), 388.
2 Alain Locke, "Negro Youth Speaks," in *The New Negro*, ed. Alain Locke. (1925; reprint, New York: Touchstone, 1992), 48.
3 Fred Moten, *Black and Blur* (Durham: Duke University Press, 2017), 85. Moten's words are "acknowledging what it is to own dispossession, which cannot be owned but by which one can be possessed" (85).
4 Alain Locke, *The New Negro* (1925; reprint, New York: Touchstone, 1992), 48.
5 Jean Fagan Yellin, Harriet Jacobs: A Life (New York: Basic Civitas Books, 2004), 122.

Introduction: The Affective Atmosphere of African American Literature

6   Walter Benn Michaels, *The Shape of the Signifier: From 1967 to the End of History* (Princeton, 2004), 113.
7   Gwendolyn Brooks, "Poets Who Are Negroes," *Phylon* (1940–1956), Vol. 11, No. 4 (4th Qtr., 1950), 312.
8   Ralph Ellison, Invisible Man (New York: Vintage Books, 1995 [1952]), 438.
9   Robert Stepto, in *Afro-American Literature: The Reconstruction of Instruction*, argues that 1970s survey courses of African American literature use the literature as a springboard for a discussion of the "non-literary." He emphasizes "the simple, haunting fact that Afro-American history and social science are being taught while Afro-American language, literature, and literacy are not" (9).
    Dexter Fisher and Robert B. Stepto, ed. *Afro-American Literature: The Reconstruction of Instruction* (New York: The Modern Language Association of America, 1979), 9.
10 Raymond Williams, *The Sociology of Culture* (Chicago: University of Chicago, 1981), viii.
11 Michael Boyce Gillespie, Film Blackness: American Cinema and the Idea of Black Film (Durham: Duke University, 2016).
12 Alexis Pauline Gumbs and Mattilda Bernstein Sycamore, "We Are Always Crossing: Alexis Pauline Gumbs," *Bomb*, 22 March 2018.
13 Fawz Kabra, "Interview with John Akomfrah" July 5, 2018. *Ocula.com*
14 Amiri Baraka, 'Technology & Ethos" in *Raise Rage Rays Raze: Essays Since 1965* (New York: Random House, 1971)
15 Alexis Pauline Gumbs, *M Archive: After the End of the World* (Durham and London: Duke University Press, 2018), 51.
16 Ashon T. Crawley, *Blackpentecostal Breath: The Aesthetics of Possibility* (New York: Fordham University Press, 2017), 52–53.
17 Walker writes, "*Cane* was for Toomer a double 'swan song.' He meant it to memorialize a culture he thought was dying, whose folk spirit he considered beautiful, but he was also saying goodbye to the "Negro" he felt dying in himself. *Cane* then is a parting gift, and no less precious because of that. I think Jean Toomer would want us to keep its beauty, but let him go" (65). Alice Walker, *In Search of Our Mothers' Gardens* (Orlando: Harcourt Inc., 1983)
18 Darby English, *How to See a Work of Art in Total Darkness* (Cambridge: Massachusetts Institute of Technology Press, 2010)

19 "Richard Wright Describes the Birth of *Black Boy*," *New York Post*, 30 November 1944, B6.
20 Michael Warner's theory in *Publics and Counterpublics* (2005).
21 Book cover quote, Middleton A. Harris, *The Black Book* (New York: Random House, 1974)
22 Ibid., preface, unpaginated.
23 *In Our Terribleness*, unpaginated.
24 Jacques Derrida, "Signature, Event, Context" in *Margins of Philosophy*, trans. Alan Bass (Chicago: University of Chicago Press, 1985)
25 Andrei Gorea, "Thoughts on Specific Nerve Energies." Representations of Vision: Trends and Tacit Assumptions in Vision Research, ed. Andrei Gorea (Cambridge: Cambridge University Press, 1991), 219–230.
26 Toni Morrison, *Beloved* (New York: Vintage, 2004), 61.
27 Ameer Baraka (Amiri Baraka), "We Are Our Feeling: The Black Aesthetic" (*Negro Digest*, September 1969), 5.
28 Fredric Jameson, *The Antinomies of Realism* (London & New York: Verso, 2013), 76.
29 Jonathan Flatley, "Reading for Mood," Representations, Vol. 140, No. 1, Fall 2017, pp. 137–158.

1

The Textual Production of Black Affect: The Blush of Toni Morrison's Last Novel

The most successful fiction of most Negro writing is in its emotional content.
                    Amiri Baraka, "The Myth of a 'Negro Literature'"

For within living structures defined by profit, by linear power, by institutional dehumanization, our feelings were not meant to survive.
                    Audre Lorde, "Poetry is not a Luxury"

The idea was always to make that time emotionally real to people.
                    –Octavia Butler[1]

In "Toni Morrison on a Book She Loves," Morrison explains how Gayl Jones' novel *Corregidora* (1975) transformed African American women's literature. As Morrison remembers her first encounter of *Corregidora*, she foregrounds the textual production of affect (a "smile of disbelief" that she still "feels on her mouth" two years after reading Jones' manuscript). Morrison writes:

What is African American Literature?, First Edition. Margo N. Crawford.
© 2021 John Wiley & Sons, Inc. Published 2021 by John Wiley & Sons, Inc.

> What was uppermost in my mind while I read her manuscript was that no novel about any black woman could ever be the same after this ... So deeply impressed was I that I hadn't time to be offended by the fact that she was twenty-four and had no "right" to know so much so well... Even now, almost two years later, I shake my head when I think of her, and the same smile of disbelief I could not hide when I met her, I feel on my mouth still as I write these lines...[2]

Affect differs from conscious feeling and voluntary body response. Toni Morrison's lingering smile, produced by Gayl Jones' *Corregidora*, is an example of the textual production of uncontainable and unexplainable black feeling that this chapter analyzes. When African American literature produces affective experiences such as what is "felt on the mouth," the is-ness of the literature is a particular sticky tension. Sara Ahmed's attention to the stickiness of affect is similar to what Morrison expresses when she remembers the impact of *Corregidora* as a lingering sensation felt on her mouth. Ahmed proposes, in *The Cultural Politics of Emotion*, that "objects become sticky, or saturated with affect, as sites of personal and social tension" (11). Morrison experiences *Corregidora* as such a sticky book. In a similar sense, Gayl Jones, in an interview, offers a theory of the role of stickiness and tension in the very meaning of "legacy" in African American literary studies. As Jones thinks about Zora Neale Hurston's literary influence, she foregrounds the tensions that Hurston produced–"We have to do something about the tensions that she had. [...] That's what legacy is."[3]

On the lower frequencies, what are the sticky tensions of African American literature? The black protest of *The Nation*'s decision, in 2018, to publish Anders Carlson-Wee's poem "How-To" reveals the complexity of the sticky tensions. Carlson-Wee, a white poet, assumes the voice of a homeless person in this poem. Some black readers felt an attempt to approach the sonic waves of an African American vernacular. These readers protested *The Nation* editors' choice to publish this poem when so few black poets are published in *The Nation*. These readers were offended by what felt, to them, like cultural appropriation and a caricature of Black English.

The Textual Production of Black Affect

The poet, Carlson-Wee, apologized publicly (on social media) and asserted, "Treading anywhere close to blackface is horrifying to me, and I am profoundly regretful." Whether one feels the proximity of his poem to blackface may depend on how black (or not necessarily black) the words (and the gestures to nonverbal affect) feel. The poem reads:

> If you got hiv, say aids. If you a girl,/say you're pregnant—nobody gonna lower/themselves to listen for the kick. People/passing fast. Splay your legs, cock a knee/funny. It's the littlest shames they're likely/to comprehend. Don't say homeless, they know/you is. What they don't know is what opens/a wallet, what stops em from counting/what they drop. If you're young say younger./Old say older. If you're crippled don't/flaunt it. Let em think they're good enough/Christians to notice. Don't say you pray,/say you sin. It's about who they believe/they is. You hardly even there.[4]

The words "nobody gonna lower themselves to listen for the kick" capture the tension between reading this poem and feeling a specifically black dialect and reading this poem and feeling the lack of (or an appropriation of) black affect. Are the words "to listen for the kick" only felt as a gesture to black affect if someone has felt the kick of a black text being born and felt there is something private about this strange affective property, something as unconscious and involuntary as the kick of the not-yet-here? The words "you hardly even there" may open up the most intriguing part of black readers' protest of *The Nation*'s decision to publish this poem. The protestors may have read those final words and felt a desire for black "thereness."

A crucial moment in Frederick Douglass' iconic slave narrative *Narrative of the Life of Frederick Douglass: An American Slave Written by Himself* (1845) sheds light on the feeling of "black thereness" that shapes the idea of African American literature. Douglass writes:

> I was seldom whipped by my old master, and suffered little from any thing else than hunger and cold. I suffered much from hunger, but much more from cold. In hottest summer and coldest winter, I was

> kept almost naked—no shoes, no stockings, no jacket, no trousers, nothing on but a coarse tow linen shirt, reaching only to my knees. I had no bed. I must have perished with cold, but that, the coldest nights, I used to steal a bag which was used for carrying corn to the mill. I would crawl into this bag, and there sleep on the cold, damp, clay floor, with my head in and feet out. My feet have been so cracked with the frost, that the pen with which I am writing might be laid in the gashes.[5]

Putting the "pen in the gashes" would suspend the writing. To know that feeling, Douglass would have to stop writing and linger, suspended, in the space between writing and bodily feeling. The idea of African American literature "might be laid" in the gap between words and a "fever-chart of affects and intensities rising and falling" (Fredric Jameson's lucid description, in *The Antinomies of Realism*, of the affective energy that cannot be mapped by narrative).

Douglass' image of the pen that "might be laid in the gashes" takes us to the tension between the personal and impersonal that shapes affect. Douglass uses this image to underscore the bodily effects of having to endure the brutal cold. But the friction between the pen and the gash signals the zone where the writing instrument cannot be separated from the black body. Douglass' pen "might be laid" in his body and the body of African American literature. The pen that might be laid in the gashes might create the idea of African American literature. Any approach to African American literature as the art tied to an inevitable, collective black identity must take account of Douglass' "might be" approach to the notion of putting the pen in the gashes. A "gash" is a "long deep slash, cut, or wound." The practice of African American literature might be the gestures toward the cuts that create the shared slash of blackness.

Thomas Jefferson's diminishing of Phillis Wheatley's practice of cutting and slashing lingers. He sees Wheatley and any black writer as being unable to rise above narration in order to produce art. He writes, "Never yet could I find a Black that had uttered a thought above the level of plain narration; never seen even an elementary trait of painting or sculpture."[6] What *is* African American literature? It is "above the level of plain narration." The is-ness may be what Toni Morrison, in *Jazz*, imagines as the "severed parts [trying to] remember the snatch."[7] The is-ness may be what is produced by the ongoing attempts to touch and know a collective loss, a "snatch," that cannot ever be known. The paratexts of slave narratives (that needed those authenticating words "written by himself" and "written by herself") made the idea of African American literature, from its origins, a brand (a brand that should never have become a brand). The is-ness of African American literature is the refusal to remain the brand of "I write myself into existence." The is-ness is the shared atmosphere of unapologetic black existence.

In a dialogue with Claudia Rankine, Lauren Berlant proposes that *Citizen* pulls readers into a "collective nervous system."[8] Just as Rankine's *Citizen* is the textual production of this collective nervous system, many other texts in the African American literary tradition pull readers into a collective nervous system as the textual production performs the "shared atmosphere" of affect. Paratexts such as the cover of Langston Hughes and Roy DeCarava's *The Sweet Flypaper of Life* (1955) perform the shared atmosphere of an open book as the first words of the text appear on the cover. The book cover also includes the words "continued on page 3." The reading begins on the surface; the outer and the inner collapse and put the reader in a shared atmosphere in which the reader's eyes and the eyes in Roy DeCarava's photograph meet in the space of the embodied and the disembodied, the mix of conscious and unconscious gazes as the actual eye meets the eye in the photograph. The imprint of a kiss on the cover of Jayne Cortez's poetry volume *Mouth on Paper* (1977) is another vivid example of the textual production of a shared atmosphere of affect (between eyes, mouth, and paper) as reading the cover hails the kissing of the cover and a body/text affective tension.

Figure 2.

Figure 3.

The Textual Production of Black Affect

In "Feeling, Emotion, Affect," Eric Shouse develops a theory of affect that lends itself beautifully to the role of black affect in shaping the idea of African American literature. He writes:

> The power of affect lies in the fact that it is unformed and unstructured (abstract). It is affect's "abstractivity" that makes it transmittable in ways that feelings and emotions are not, and it is because affect is transmittable that it is potentially such a powerful social force. This is why it is important not to confuse affect with feelings and emotions, and why I agree with Brian Massumi that Lawrence Grossberg's term 'affective investments' doesn't make a whole lot of sense. If, as Massumi proposes, affect is "unformed and unstructured," and it is always prior to and/or outside of conscious awareness, how is one to 'invest' in it? Investment presumes forethought and a site for deposit, and affect precedes thought and is as stable as electricity.[9]

African American literature is not a "site of deposit" of black affect; it is the flow of affective energies. It is the instability of black electricity.

We feel this electricity when Olaudah Equiano, in *The Interesting Narrative of the Life of Olaudah Equiano*, writes, "I have often seen my master and Dick employed in reading; and I had a great curiosity to talk to the books, as I thought they did; and so to learn how all the things had a beginning: for that purpose I have often taken up a book, and have talked to it, and then put my ears to it, when alone in hopes it would answer me; and I have been very much concerned when I found it remained silent."[10] Equiano's words "put my ears to it" gesture to the brush of the ear on the book, the press of the ear on the book, and other affective exchanges that shape this moment of trying to feel the is-ness of a book. When Toni Morrison, at the end of *Jazz*, writes, "Look where your hands are. Now," we hear a similar move to the body and text interaction, but Morrison also moves to a zone of what is outside of conscious awareness (229). We blush when these words ("Look where your hands are. Now.") make us wonder what our hands are doing.

What is African American Literature?

Toni Morrison's *Blush*

God Help the Child (2015), the last novel Morrison published during her lifetime, enacts the shock that occurs when the is-ness of African American literature is nothing but an unapologetic depiction of black life, rendered on its own terms with no need to explain. God help the child who knows how to understand this novel. The novel is hard to *handle*. The character Sweetness, in *God Help the Child*, might make us cringe when she confesses her inability to love her daughter, Lula Ann (Bride), or she may make us *blush*. Our partial understanding of her shock at having the very dark-skinned child may turn our shock at her inability to even want to touch her child into more of a blush. Morrison refuses, in this last novel, to create a sad or tragic mood as she tells a story about colorism. As shame meets shock, black readers (who have internalized and fought the internalization of colorism) blush as we read the trauma without the anchor of a melancholy mood. Morrison's interest in colorism evolves, from *The Bluest Eye* to *Tar Baby* to *Paradise* and *God Help the Child*. In *Paradise* (1997), as Morrison approaches the twenty-first century, she begins to develop the unmarking (the loosening) of colorism trauma that emerges most fully in her only novel set in the twenty-first century, *God Help the Child* (2015). In *Paradise*, the theory of 8-rock and the theory of the "open body" are at the core of her emergent practice of loosening thick time and unmarking the flesh that we call the black body. Morrison describes the open body as a template, a silhouette, of the body. Throughout *Paradise*, Morrison meditates on semiotics and her idea of open body becomes a part of this larger theorizing about marks scattered throughout the novel. During Reverend Misner's interior monologue as he holds a cross in front of a congregation, he thinks about the cross as the "original mark embedded in consciousness as consciousness itself" (145). Misner's internal, unspoken sermon on the original mark is a meditation on the primalness of the sign of the cross, the omnipresence of the cross as an original mark upon which so many other forms, such as the face, are built. Morrison writes, "It was this mark, this, that lay underneath every other" (145-6). The discourse of the original mark has a surface/depth tension that reshapes underneathness into the deep presence of a surface. The cross is "embedded in consciousness as consciousness itself," as if Morrison is looking for a new grammar that allows "consciousness" to be conceptual surface, not conceptual depth. Misner holds the cross as he stands, silently, in front of the congregation as if he wants the cross to speak for itself, as if he wants the cross to be looked at and not looked through.

Reverend Misner would understand Stephen Best and Sharon Marcus' description of surface reading:

> Surface becomes […] less a layer that conceals, as clothing does skin, or encloses, as a building's facade does its interior, than what is evident, perceptible, apprehensible in texts; what is neither hidden nor hiding; what, in the geometrical sense, has length and breadth but no thickness, and therefore covers no depth. A surface is what insists on being looked *at* rather than what we must train ourselves to see *through*.[11]

The practice of surface, in *Paradise*, is tied to the practice of refusing the 8-rock rule of the reproduction of unadulterated black "bloodlines." Morrison makes the "original mark" the surface alternative to the imagined depth of "8-rock" blackness. Reverend Misner's unspoken sermon on the "original mark" begs to be compared to Consolata's art therapy of the "open body." The women's marking of the outlines of their bodies on the cellar floor, this art therapy of feeling less marked through the process of marking the shape of one's body, shows Morrison's interest in the tension between marks that become signs of race and gender and marks that remain marks and do not have to gain the depth of identity tied to race and gender.

What is African American Literature?

In *Paradise*, the marking of dark-skinned blackness deepens into the 8-rock feeling of the need to not taint "deep" blackness. This deep blackness is conveyed through the 8-rock reference to the coal mines. Depth is written onto skin color through this imagining of a community that cherishes "blue-blackness" and feels that their skin color is a sign of the depth of their lineage, collective history, and the prosperity of their all-black town, Ruby. In this novel, as Morrison depicts the 8-rockers, she strains to understand this impulse to feel this thick time of skin and she also strains, as she depicts the women who live outside of this all-black town, to find access to a loosening of this thick time. She finds this access to this loosening in the images of the open body art therapy. Morrison uses Consolata and the Convent women to imagine an example of a "severed part remember[ing] the snatch, the slice of its disfigurement" (*Jazz*, 159). Indeed, the narrator explains that the Convent women, "in spite of or because their bodies ache," enter the "dreamer's tale," in which their body silhouettes on the cellar floor gain "muscle and bone" (264, 159). Their aching bodies, or "severed parts," literally "remember the snatch" when they lie on the floor of the cellar and Consolata paints templates of their bodies. It is most apparent that they are "born again" when the revision of the opening of the Book of Genesis appears: "In the beginning the most important thing was the template" (263). In the description of the open body, the act of unmarking the body through the marking of the body templates is comparable to the *body work* needed to undo what Morrison, in *The Source of Self-Regard*, posits as the linking of "slavebody" (rendered as one word, a body eternally marked as "slave") and the "blackbody" (rendered as one word, a body eternally marked as "black").

As Bakhtin develops the idea of the chronotope, he writes, "time, as it were, thickens, takes on flesh."[12] The thickening of time and time's "taking on of flesh," in terms of the afterlife of slavery, gain new dimensions when we rethink Fanon's theory of epidermalization – "the slow composition of my *self* as a body in the middle of a spatial and temporal world." The slow *decomposition* of the black body as a slave body demands a loosening of the thickness of that melancholic historicism that keeps collapsing black past and black present. Morrison's body work in Baby Suggs' sermon on flesh includes the moment of "women letting loose." The text reads:

> Finally she called the women to her. 'Cry,' she told them. 'For the living and the dead. Just cry.' And without covering their eyes the women let loose.
>
> It started that way: laughing children, dancing men, crying women and then it got mixed up. Women stopped crying and danced; men sat down and cried; children danced, women laughed, children cried until, exhausted and riven, all and each lay about the Clearing damp and gasping for breath (103).

The letting loose (described immediately before the now iconic call for black love of black flesh) is the necessary state of rivenness that enables Suggs' outdoor congregation to be open enough to move from black body to flesh. This body work in *Beloved*, like the body work in *Paradise*, is a gearing up for the body work in *God Help the Child*.

In *God Help the Child*, Toni Morrison claims a way of talking about black bodies that is radically different from the focus on black embodiment in her first novel *The Bluest Eye*. Her last and her first novel both focus on colorism and the formative childhood trauma shaped by colorism, but, in *God Help the Child*, the Fanonian "Look, a Negro!" trauma is reshaped into the tension between the social logic of racial self-hatred and the lived experience of shaking off and interrupting the corporeal enactment of this self-hatred. The novel should make us pause and think more about the difference between the Fanonian "slow composition of my self as a body in the middle of a spatial and temporal world" and Morrison's theory of the "open body" (developed in her novel *Paradise*).[13] The open body is the lived experience of feeling that one is marked and unmarked, touched and untouched. In "Eye to Eye: black women, hatred, and anger" (in *Sister Outsider*, 1984), Audre Lorde dramatizes the affective energy that creates the tension between the open body of blackened subjects and the social logic of the always already marked black body. Lorde writes:

> When I look up the woman is still staring at me, her nose holes and eyes huge. And suddenly I realise that there is nothing crawling up the seat between us; it is me she doesn't want her coat to touch. The fur brushes past my face as she stands with a shudder and holds on to a strap in the speeding train ... Something's going on here I do not understand, but I will never forget it. Her eyes. The flared nostrils. The hate (147).

The affect in this passage is so pronounced – the brush of fur "past" face and the shudder. Clare Hemmings argues that Lorde presents "a different affective trajectory than the one that would deny her subjectivity."[14] Lorde's image of the "fur brushing past my face as she stands with a shudder" makes the affective exchange between the white person who stares and the black person being stared at seem like a transfer of energy that is too much of a shudder to be felt within any discourse that reshapes shudders into more stable, legible ways of talking about the racialized body (the corporeal enactment of race).

In *God Help the Child*, Morrison makes black *shudder* (black release) matter more than the marking of black bodily trauma. The shudder has a way of unmarking the marked body. Lyrics by Young M.A perform this shudder: *"These haters on my body shake 'em off."* Morrison's last novel is the shaking off of the colorism that sticks in *The Bluest Eye*, her first novel. In *God Help the Child*, Morrison depicts black embodiment as the subject in the process of being transformed into an object. The body work in *God Help the Child* pivots on passages that present the wiggling of toes and smiling at one's lipstick stain on a glass. The subject/object tension differs greatly from the Fanonian "Look, a Negro" "object among other

The Textual Production of Black Affect

objects" discourse in *The Bluest Eye*. The description of Soaphead Church, in *The Bluest Eye*, begs to be compared to an image, in *God Help the Child*, of Bride's wiggling toes and smiling at her lipstick imprint. The fraudulent spiritual advisor Soaphead Church who tells the wounded, dark-skinned child Pecola that he will give her blue eyes is described in the following manner: "The residue of the human spirit smeared on inanimate objects was all he could withstand of humanity" (163). The lived experience of blackness in *The Bluest Eye* is the "residue of the human spirit smeared on inanimate objects." In *God Help the Child*, Morrison subtly but powerfully depicts the lived experiences of black subjects interacting with vibrant things. Here is the *God Help the Child* passage that defies *The Bluest Eye* image of black smeared residue of human spirit: "Wiggling my toes under the silk cushion I couldn't help smiling at the lipstick smile on my wineglass" (11).

God Help the Child may be Morrison's intentionally "off" novel, the novel that may call for a reading that allows surface to remain surface. The pleasure of the book may be the fact that the characters remain "surface" so that the trauma depicted is not felt as we might feel it in her earlier novels. The twenty-first century intervention of this first book set in the twenty-first century may be the idea that African American literature can be slippery. Remember the final words in *Jazz*: "Look where your hands are. Now." *God Help the Child* makes us feel, "You can't touch this. You can't really hold this."

But maybe *you can feel it*. For example, when you hear Bride in her *first* first person narration, say, "I couldn't help smiling at the lipstick smile on my wineglass, (11), you may blush if you think about the sensation that is finding words and turning into a certain *feeling* in this passage. The lipstick lingers on the glass, without any lipstick wearer intending to leave an imprint. The press of the lips creates the mark. Bride says, "I couldn't help smiling at the lipstick smile." The involuntary nature of the smile reminds us that Morrison is indeed moving to the affect that is more unformed and abstract than feelings. This image in the novel makes me think about black women's marking of surfaces that are not, as Eric Shouse writes, "a site for deposit." The marking on the edge of the surface signals such a difference from the often-cited "eruptions of funk" language in *The Bluest Eye*.

Morrison foregrounds the lips in both the iconic passage describing the eruptions of funk, in *The Bluest Eye*, and in the image of Bride, in *God Help the Child*, looking at the lipstick imprint on the glass. The fear of the eruptions of funk is described in the following manner:

> Wherever it erupts, this Funk, they wipe it away; where it crusts, they dissolve it: wherever it drips, flowers, or clings, they find it and fight it until it dies. They fight this battle all the way to the grave. The laugh that is a little too loud; the enunciation a little too round; the gesture a little too generous. They hold their behind in for fear of a sway too free; when they wear lipstick, they never cover the entire mouth for fear of lips too thick, and they worry, worry, worry about the edges of their hair. (83)

Scholars have done so much with this quintessential Morrrison phrase "the eruptions of funk." When we connect *God Help the Child* and *The Bluest Eye* and foreground the issue of the privileging of surface and black affect, in *God Help the Child*, over the melancholic depth in *The Bluest Eye*, *God Help the Child* is Morrison's twenty-first century "eruption of funk," her twenty-first century putting on of all of the overstated lipstick that Bride would never wear (with her flawless fashion sense). *God Help the Child* is then the intentionally "off" novel that is not striving for the eloquence and form of *A Mercy*, *Beloved*, and other novels written by her. *God Help the Child* is a little raw, but this rawness is only a flaw as Kara Walker claims (in her 2015 review in *The New York Times*) if we fail to truly feel the funk, the sensations beneath the words, beneath the unapologetic surface. Morrison, echoing Sweetness' words, seems to say, "It's not my fault," if I want to write a different kind of novel.

At the very end of *God Help the Child*, we learn how to read Sweetness and how to read the play with surface and black affect throughout the entire novel. When Sweetness mocks the way people greet newborns and perform the bliss of the mother-child affair,

Morrison uses language that foregrounds Teresa Brennan's sense that "feelings are sensations that have found a match in words" (19). Sweetness, as she imagines that she is talking directly to Bride, says:

> Good move, Lulu Ann. If you think mothering is all cooing, booties, and diapers you're in for a big shock. Big. You and your nameless boyfriend, husband, pickup—whoever—imagine OOOH! A baby! Kitchee kitchee koo!
> Listen to me. You are about to find out what it takes, how the world is, how it works and how it changes when you are a parent.
> Good luck and God help the child. (178)

The "baby talk" is a fascinating way to think about the words that are not really words, the unformed affect, and sensations, that are bursting out of the normative bubble trying to enclose and erase the pain that Sweetness knows, the pain tied to this flesh that we might call a body. In this end of this novel, Morrison shifts to Sweetness' *unspeakable* pain, after the fuller novel has shown us Bride's tremendous move to the pleasure of this flesh that we might call a body. After Sweetness' mocking of the baby talk, her mocking of the words that are so phony as they try to name the sensations of reproductive joy, Sweetness says "*Listen* to me," before we get the title words "God Help the Child."

Sweetness' final (conscious or unconscious) "God Help the Child" gesture to *listening* to Billie Holiday echoes even more when we remember Amiri Baraka's tribute, in *Black Music*, to this "dark lady of the sonnets." The holding in, at the very end of the novel (Sweetness not saying what she could say or not being able to find the words that would begin to match what she feels about "how the world is"), is similar to Billie Holiday's affect as described by Baraka in his tribute. Baraka writes, "More than I have I felt to say, she says always. More than she has ever felt is what we mean by fantasy. Emotion, is wherever you are. She stayed in the street." Baraka's focus on affect here ties so beautifully to what I think Morrison is really doing in *God Help the Child*. Baraka's sense that "emotion, is wherever you are" takes us to the zone of affect that is too abstract and unstructured to be treated as a conscious feeling. When Sweetness unconsciously or consciously leans on Billie Holiday's song "God Bless the Child," as she tries to "keep it real," she, like Billie Holiday, refuses to convert "street knowledge" into the pie in the sky "Kitchee kitchee koo!" language that she mocks immediately before she imagines that she is talking directly to Bride and says, "Listen to me. You are about to find out what it takes, how the world is, and how it works and changes when you are a parent" (178).

Late style Morrison shows us that she does not want to be treated as some type of sacred mother of African American literature, or African American women's literature. Forget the "kitchee kitchee koo!," she may be telling us. Let me feel what I want to feel as I move from recent statements that sound like distancing myself from the category "African American literature" to the grain of my late style, and early style voice, that holds on to black affect. Baraka, in his tribute to Holiday, writes, "Nothing was more perfect that what she was. Nor more willing to fail. (if we call failure something light can realize. Once you have seen it, or felt whatever thing she conjured growing in your flesh.)" Kara Walker and others' sense of the failed, *late style* novel should simply make us, remembering Baraka's words, consider the productive nature of failure and our affective responses to this failure that cannot be explained easily as we try to say this is how *God Help the Child* made me feel.

In her foreword in the book *The Black Photographers Annual 1973* (published by the Black Photographers Annual, Inc.), Morrison explains her "early style" understanding of the textual production of black affect, in the following manner. She writes:

> This is a rare book: not only because it is a first, but also because it is an original idea complemented by enormous talent, energy and some of the most powerful and poignant photography I have ever seen. It was conceived as a commitment to the community of Black artists, executed as a glorious display of their craft and their perception. Consequently it is an ideal publishing venture, combining as it does necessity and beauty, pragmatism and art.

It is also a true book. It hovers over the matrix of black life, takes accurate aim and explodes our sensibilities. [...]

Not only is it a true book, it is a free book. It is beholden to no elaborate Madison Avenue force. [...] There is no higher praise for any project than that it is rare, true, and free. And isn't that what art is all about? And isn't that what we are all about?[15]

In the *early style* zone of Morrison, we see her sense that what makes a book "black" is its commitment to a non-Madison Avenue force and black community and, also, its ability to, somehow, remain a "free book." In her May 1975 lecture at Portland State University, she continues to search for this language that makes the notion of an ideal black readership a way of being "both free and situated" (her words in the essay "Home," 1997). In one transcription of the Portland State lecture, she asserts, "When Black writers write, they should write for me. There is very little literature that's really like that, Black literature. I don't mean that it wasn't necessary to have the other kind. Richard Wright is not talking to me. Or even you. He's talking to some White people. He's explaining something to them. [...] And I know when they're talking just past my ear, when they're explaining something, justifying something, just defining something. [Glass thunks.]"

The sensation of the glass "thunking" is the black affect that Morrison, *early style*, wants to see translated into words. Later, in this same lecture, Morrison refers to writing "for all those people in the book who don't even pick up the book.... all those non-readers, all those people in Sula who (a) don't exist and (b) if they did wouldn't buy it anyway. But they are the ones to whom one speaks. Not to the New York Times; not to the editors; not to any distant media; not to anything. It is very private thing. They are the ones who say, 'Yeah, uh huh, that's right.'" This peculiar, puzzling sense of writing to an ideal reader *who does not exist* shows, that like the inclusion of the "uh huh," Morrison is searching for words that begin to explain her investment in black affect. Remembering Morrison's glass thunk, after all those words, reminds us that Morrison, like Billie Holiday, was also calling for an end of the need to explain.[16]

It is hard to explain the significance of the depictions of affective exchanges between people and objects in *God Help the Child*. Consider again these images (of a person's smile interacting with the lipstick imprint of a smile on a wine glass, the image of Bride and Booker's spines interacting with the car seats' "soft hide of cattle" (175), and repeated image of Booker's shaving brush rubbing against Bride's skin). Morrison makes the friction between people and surfaces matter as the tension between surface and depth becomes the prime theme of the novel. *God Help the Child*'s non-binary rethinking of the interplay between surface and depth takes us back to Morrison's description, in her essay "The Site of Memory," of her work as a writer. She writes, "It is emotional memory—what the nerves and skin remember" (99). Could it be that the entire novel is an attempt to make readers slide around on the *surface* that the novel becomes, with the characters who are intentionally "less developed" than characters in her other novels. In the process of teaching us how to slide around the issues that, in *The Bluest Eye*, made us want to cry, could it be that Morrison, in her one and only novel set in the twenty-first century, is opening up African American literature to that which Fredric Jameson describes as that "fever-chart of affects and intensities rising and falling" (76).

Reading *God Help the Child*, we have to do what Florens, in *A Mercy*, demands that the blacksmith do, if he wants to learn how to "read" the words she is carving on the wall. We have to bend down and shape our body around the words. In *A Mercy*, Florens tells the blacksmith, "[Y]ou will have to bend down to read my telling, crawl perhaps in a few places" (185). These words beg to be compared to the last words in *Jazz*: "Look where your hands are. Now." Morrison depicts reading as touching a text that touches us. Once we learn how to read this novel as a dramatizing of the touching and being touched relation between people and surfaces, many layers of the novel gain new dimensions. The fact that Sweetness cannot bear to touch her young daughter (due to the colorism, the ideology, written on the body) dramatizes how touch might shatter the intactness of ideology.

The Textual Production of Black Affect

As the title of the novel clings to Billie Holiday, Morrison takes us back to the difference between Carl Van Vechten's photograph of Billie Holiday carefully, delicately holding an African sculpture as she looks at it and Van Vechten's photograph of Billie Holiday's face touching the sculpture that is touching her. "Listen to me" as Sweetness says, so simply, in *God Help the Child*, could be a call to "touch and be touched" (as Zora Neale Hurston writes in *Their Eyes Were Watching God*, "come kiss and be kissed"). Sweetness' mantra, at the beginning and the end of the opening section of the novel, is: "It's not my fault. So you can't blame me." Morrison overemphasizes Sweetness' refusal of blame: "Her color is a cross she will always carry. But it's not my fault. It's not my fault. It's not my fault. It's not" (7). These words stick and push the fault outward. In *Song of Solomon*, Morrison, in one scene describing Milkman, writes, "something like shame stuck to his skin" (418). This idea of shame that sticks contrasts greatly with the move, in *God Help the Child*, to the blame that cannot stick to the black subject and, in the depiction of Bride, the shame that cannot stick. In contrast to Sweetness' sense that "her color is a cross she will always carry," Bride's color becomes her pleasure, joy, and literal currency. As she becomes a well-off executive in the fashion and beauty industry, Bride wears white every day, white that accentuates the glow of dark skin. Morrison, in her only novel that is set in the twenty-first century, denaturalizes the melancholy tied to "carrying" the dark skin that is the starting point (*The Bluest Eye*) of her trajectory of novels. The shame that sticks to Milkman's skin is also the shame that "sticks" to *The Bluest Eye* when we first open the book and feel the weight of the "Dick and Jane" primers that feel so "white."

We open *God Help the Child* and we might feel the production of a black interiority in Sweetness' opening words "It's not my fault." If we hear black sound in these opening words, it is black sound that cannot be analyzed as some type of telling, signature black vernacular. If we hear this black interiority, it is an interiority projected onto a surface that is just surface. "It's not my fault" does not have the black vernacular depth embedded in the opening words "Quiet as it's kept," in *The Bluest Eye*. In "Unspeakable Things Unspoken," Morrison gives such an extensive analysis of her reasons for beginning this first novel with the words "Quiet as it's kept."

I am struck by the difference between this focus on the forced, necessary interiority (and the careful way that Morrison explains how "Quiet as it's kept" is a "familiar phrase" "tied to black women conversing with one another") and the way we really could not analyze "It's not my fault" with such detail and care. We slide over these opening words in *God Help the Child*. This slippery opening is similar to Morrison's depiction of beauty as slippery. In a 2015 interview with Toni Morrison, Griffin confesses, "I have to be self-indulgent. I know that skin color and beauty is superficial but I for one was so grateful for a jet-black character who is gorgeous and stunning. Why do you do that? Give it to me and snatch it back?" Morrison's response shows how she, in her signature twenty-first century novel, is producing black blush. Morrison tells Griffin, "Sudanese black, as her mother calls them, …And they have these exquisite faces, I mean unbelievable. Anyway where was I? …The point is that neither one will help you… I'd rather not be ugly, just to get through the street, but it's more important to be a three dimensional person… Even when it was the glorious, glorious beauty of a glorious black woman. It ain't enough." The blush that may happen when we hear Morrison, our elder, lose her train of thought as she remembers being smitten by Sudanese beauty, may be similar to the way that we blush as we realize that Morrison, in this last novel, delivers the unapologetic mother figure who remains too indifferent to feel the shame that readers expect her to feel (shame for not wanting to touch her dark-skinned child and shame for feeling too "high yellow" to give birth to a dark-skinned child).

In *God Help the Child*, indifference is the mood of the novel and the form of the novel once the character development becomes too unformed to matter as much as the larger emotional flow of the novel. Morrison refuses to create a straightforward portrait of racial self-hatred. Like Kara Walker's recent *shadow* image of Morrison, *God Help the Child*, this last novel, is a bold

The Textual Production of Black Affect

letting go of any investment in portraiture. Walker, as she explains the image on *The New Yorker* cover, insists, "I'm no portraitist, but I am a shadow maker." The thick time of slave past equals black present is what Kara Walker's silhouettes complicate. Walker's landscape silhouettes dramatize what Calvin Warren, in "Black Time: Slavery, Metaphysics, and the Logic of Wellness," describes as the "event horizon" of slavery. Walker's event horizon is not the thick time that gives us Fanon's "slow composition of my *self* as a body in the middle of a spatial and temporal world," what Fanon delivers as the body's wearing of the heavy "historicity." As Walker continues to make silhouette forms decenter the impulse to see recognizable bodies, she moves from her 2019 thick sculpture of Morrison to the 2019 lighter cut-out, silhouette form that appears on *The New Yorker* cover. The silhouette emerges after the work done through the sculpture. The silhouette is closer to the fleeting shudder that Audre Lorde gives us (in "Eye to Eye" in *Sister Outsider*) in the image of what brushes past the face. In Lorde's image, this shudder time is as stinging in its lightness as the brush of the white women's fur past the black women's face (the "fur brushes past my face as she stands with a shudder"). And the brush "past my face" is unforgettable. Lorde emphasizes the impact of the fleeting time of the shudder: "Something's going on here I do not understand, but I will never forget it" (148).

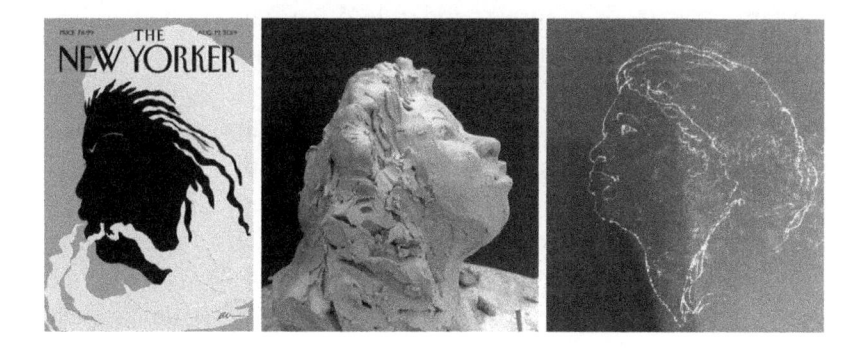

Figure 4. *The New Yorker*, Kara Walker, 2019.

What is African American Literature?

God Help the Child delivers the shudder of black subjects' often illegible lived experience of the fleeting time that does not thicken and take on flesh. The shudder time leaves bodies profoundly touched but not always already marked. Kara Walker's review of *God Help the Child* (unlike her silhouette of Morrison) refuses to grant Morrison the right to refuse to *retouch* the images of the always already marked black body. In this *New York Times* review, Walker writes, "Like Sweetness, Morrison doesn't seem to want to touch Bride either—at least not tenderly. The narrative hovers, averts its eyes and sucks its teeth at the misfortunes of the characters." Morrison's frank description of trauma, without holding it, cradling it, or fully explaining it, produces a type of readerly blush (our own shock and shame as we read, and do not touch, the trauma that she will not let us touch). Bride's mother cannot bear to touch Bride when she is a child because she recoils from what seems to have always already marked her as bound to have a hard, thick life of black trauma. Bride's ongoing fascination with the aliveness of objects that retain the touch of Booker occurs alongside images of Bride's body literally becoming less marked by thickness as she loses weight and gains a strange surface smoothness as her ear piercings close and her pubic hair disappears with a total erasure different from any waxing or shaving.

During the thick time of the Black Arts Movement, Amiri Baraka writes, "You can put on new clothes," as he hails the substance, the depth, of surface and style. When Morrison imagines this character, Bride, who puts on white clothing every day in order to become the exotic dark-skinned beauty, *the putting on of new clothes* is the act of seeming freedom (not the type of clothes put on, not what Baraka sees, as the clothing that signals black freedom). The putting on of white clothes opens up Morrison's move in this last novel to an unapologetic blackness that does not need to adhere to Baraka's insistence, in *In Our Terribleness*, that aesthetics and ideology are "the same thing." In her last novel, Morrison lets Bride's "black style" be highly commodified and too excessively surface to be interpreted through any analysis of the relation between aesthetics and ideology. We get the sense that the frustration with the inability to separate aesthetics from ideology, in *Tar Baby*, is given a new shape in *God Help the Child*. Morrison makes it impossible to read this novel through the lens of the questioning of the substance of style, as rendered in *Tar Baby*.

The limits of any investment in the substance of style is seen in *Tar Baby* when Morrison foregrounds the image of Alma Estée wearing the red wig. Morrison writes:

> So he had changed, given up fraternity, or believed he had, until he saw Alma Estée in a wig the color of dried blood. Her sweet face, her midnight skin mocked and destroyed by the pile of synthetic dried blood on her head. It was all mixed up. But he could have sorted it out if she had just stood there like a bougainvillea in a girdle, like a baby jaguar with lipstick on, like an avocado with earrings, and let him remove it. (299)

The color of the wig is described as the "color of dried blood," because, for Son, it signifies the violence of the anti-black racism underlying the dominant standards of feminine beauty. What Son imagines as the wig's mocking of Alma feels like the mocking of "his own reflection" (168). When he tries to remove the wig from Alma's head, he attempts to appropriate the body of Alma. His intention is to liberate Alma, and yet he treats her body as an object that belongs to him.

In *God Help the Child*, the white clothes (the seeming counterpart to the red wig) are devoid of the "dried blood." Morrison does not allow readers to claim any ownership of Bride's body. Just as Son cannot "sort out" Alma Estee and the red wig, the surface aura of *God Help the Child* does not encourage readers to attempt to "sort out" Bride and her white clothing. Is Bride desiring access to white affirmation through this wearing of whiteness? Morrison surely approaches this idea, but she also depicts Bride's wearing of all white as a desire for beauty (not, necessarily, whiteness). The question floating through *God Help the Child* is can we imagine the trauma of colorism (the narcissism of minor differences) losing

What is African American Literature?

its sting. If the novel seems too light, why do we expect and need the heavy story about colorism?

I was surprised when I stumbled upon pages about the Black Arts Movement in Morrison's "God Help the Child" papers at Princeton University. While Morrison was writing *God Help the Child*, she was reading a manuscript (which does not include the author's name) about the Black Arts Movement and its legacies. In between the pages of notes on *God Help the Child* and revisions of certain passages, there are these pages from a manuscript on the Black Arts Movement and its impact on later black writing. Before the many pages from this manuscript analyzing the Black Arts Movement and its legacies, the archival file on *God Help the Child* includes a two page note in which Morrison begins a tribute to Amiri Baraka, who died, in 2014, while she was writing *God Help the Child*. In this tribute to Baraka, Morrison emphasizes how she knew him since their years at Howard University and how, in her opinion, one of his most critical accomplishments was his transformation of American drama. Morrison writes, "The mourning will always be a shadow. The bright fire of his life erases it, turns it into cloud strips. [...] I've known A.B. since campus days at Howard in the 50s."[17] One of the Black Arts Movement manuscript pages refers to the "persisting interiority" of the Black Arts Movement. *God Help the Child* is a novel that has a persisting surface texture that refuses to deliver the depth of a black interior. If could be that, as Morrison was writing *God Help the Child*, she was writing alongside the archive of black interiority, not within the archive. Writing alongside the Black Arts Movement archive allows Morrison to make *God Help the Child* an unapologetically black novel that is not aiming for any recognizable black interior to recognizable black trauma. The unapologetic blackness is the impulse to not convey the shame that we expect Sweetness and other characters to feel.

Morrison meditates on this expected shame in Booker's creative writing. Booker writes:

The Textual Production of Black Affect

> I refuse to be ashamed of my shame, you know, the one assigned to me which matches the low priority and the degraded morality of those who insist upon this most facile of human feelings of inferiority and flaw simply to disguise their own cowardice by pretending it is identical to a banjo's purity. (*God Help the Child*, 150)

In the Morrison Papers in the Princeton archive (in the notes for the novel), we see that Morrison did not include some of the earlier language that would make the character Sweetness more tied to this idea of "refusing to be ashamed of my shame." In the early drafts, Sweetness is named "Dearest." Dearest, in one of these early drafts, thinks about her mistreatment of Bride (her colorism) while she is enjoying the memory of a fellow resident in the nursing home asking her to dance. The former doctor asks her to dance "just as I was about to roll back to my room." In this early draft, Sweetness reflects on what she did to her daughter as she continues to enjoy the memory of the retired doctor asking her to get out of the wheelchair and dance. Morrison writes, "and I usually stay in my wheelchair […] But just as I was about to roll back to my room a doctor – Dr—he's retired and a resident like me—asked me to dance. He's dark too—but I'm over that. I know how it hurt Lula Ann but I'm older now [aches/pains] life is too short to chop up people that way." This earlier draft adds new dimensions to the unapologetic mood of Sweetness in the novel itself. Just as Dearest/Sweetness pauses "just as she was about to roll back to her room," Morrison herself was feeling a release of the need to collect a black archive of pain as she wrote *God Help the Child*. She may have felt what she expressed at the end of her 1993 Nobel Lecture: "I trust you now. I trust you with the bird that is *not in your hands* because you have truly caught it" (italics mine).[18] In *God Help the Child*, Morrison delivers an unapologetic lack of any final redemption. The final words resonate—"Good Luck and God help the child" (178).

In an outline for *Beloved*, Morrison describes Beloved's scar as "the smile under her chin in the kootchie, kootchie koo part, that

49

is crooked and much too long." The presence of the Black Arts Movement manuscript in the *God Help the Child* papers is a tickle in the archive (the "kootchie, kootchie koo part"). In *God Help the Child*, those words "OOOH! A baby! Kitchee kitchee koo!" (in the final passage) are not entirely different from the tickle ("the kootchie, kootchie koo part") in the *Beloved* archival outline. The Black Arts Movement was on Morrison's mind as she wrote this last novel that is such a swerve from her first novel, *The Bluest Eye*, written during the Black Arts Movement. The Black Arts Movement discourse of black light opens up new dimensions of Bride's wearing of whiteness. Faith Ringgold explains the movement's "black light" in the following manner:

> In 1967 I had begun to explore the idea of a new palette, a way of expressing on canvas the new 'black is beautiful' sense of ourselves. The way we see color is influenced by the colors that surround us. Our own color for instance is indelibly etched in our mind and, unless someone tells us otherwise it influences overall sense of color. As an artist and woman of color I had become particularly interested in this idea. I had noticed that black artists tended to use a darker palette. White and Light colors are used sparingly and relegated to contrasting color in African-American, South African and East African Art. In Western art, however, white and light influence the entire palette, thereby creating a predominance of infinite, pastel colors and light and shade or chiaroscuro.[19]

When Jacques Lacan describes the process of becoming a subject as the process of "entering light," he unintentionally captures the production of racialized whiteness as *white light*.

> What determines me, at the most profound level, in the visible, is the gaze that is outside. It is through the gaze that I enter light and it is from the gaze that I receive its effects. Hence it comes about that the gaze is the instrument through which light is embodied and through which—if you will allow me to use a word, as I often do, in a fragmented form—I am *photo-graphed*.[20]

The Textual Production of Black Affect

When Bride wears the white *cover* that sets her beauty in motion, Morrison develops a new discourse of black light, one that twists the Black Arts Movement discourse of black light into a "new black" discourse of *white light as black light*. Perhaps Bride's wearing of whiteness is more than the internalization of anti-black racism, the racial self-hatred, depicted in Morrison's first novel *The Bluest Eye*. Perhaps her wearing of whiteness is her use of white light to create her own black light, not the Black Arts Movement new epistemology of light, but her own move to an unapologetic production of black beauty through an embrace of whiteness as a color, as an abstraction that she can claim and wear and use as means of *unmarking* her black body.

In her last novel, *God Help the Child*, Morrison unmarks African American literature. She defamiliarizes it. The is-ness of African American literature is what we feel when we stop looking *through* God Help the Child and look *at* it. We blush at Morrison's unapologetic move to raw affect as the only way of understanding the form of this last novel. In Kara Walker's review of the novel, she unintentionally captures the raw affect of the novel when she critiques the novel's "hovering," "averting its eyes," and suck[ing] its teeth."[21] Walker writes, "The narrative hovers, averts its eyes and sucks its teeth at the misfortunes of the characters. And like Bride, I was left hungering for warmth." This language is such a lucid description of the way that affect (the "non-conscious experience of intensity") becomes form in Morrison's last novel.[22]

Notes

1 https://inmotionmagazine.com/ac04/obutler.html
2 Toni Morrison, *What Moves at the Margin* (Jackson: University Press of Mississippi, 2008), 110.
3 Michael Harper and Robert Stepto, eds. "Gayl Jones: An Interview." *Chants of Saints: A Gathering of Afro-American Literature, Art, and Scholarship* (Urbana: University of Illinois Press, 1979), 365.

4 https://www.thenation.com/article/archive/how-to/
5 Frederick Douglass, *Narrative of the Life of Frederick Douglass* (New York: Millennium Publications, 2014), 24.
6 Henry Louis Gates, "Preface to Blackness: Text and Pretext"
7 Toni Morrison, *Jazz* (New York: Plume, 1992), 159. Morrison writes, "I will locate it so the severed part can remember the snatch, the slice of its disfigurement. Perhaps then the arm will no longer be a phantom, but will take its own shape, grow its own muscle and bone, and its blood will pump from the loud singing that has found the purpose of its serenade. Amen."
8 Lauren Berlant, "Claudia Rankine," *Bomb* 129 (Fall 2014), http://bombmagazine.org/article/10096/claudia-rankine.
9 Eric Shouse, "Feeling, Emotion, Affect," *M/C Journal* 8.6 (2005). http://journal.media-culture.org.au/0512/03-shouse.php
10 Olaudah Equiano, *The Interesting Narrative of the Life of Olaudah Equiano* (New York: Penguin, 1995 [1789]), 68.
11 Stephen Best and Sharon Marcus, "Surface Reading: An Introduction," *Representations*, Vol. 108, No. 1 (Fall 2009), 10.
12 Michael Bakhtin, *The Dialogic Imagination: Four Essays*. Trans. by C. Emerson and M. Holquist (Austin, Texas: University of Texas Press, 1981), 84.
13 Frantz Fanon, *Black Skins, White Masks*, Translated by Richard Philcox, revised ed. (New York: Grove, 2008), 91.
14 Clare Hemmings, "Invoking Affect: Cultural Theory and the Ontological Turn," *Cultural Studies* 19.5 (2005): 564.
15 Toni Morrison, *"Foreword" in The Black Photographers Annual 1973* (Brooklyn, NY: Black Photographers Annual, 1973)
16 We hear this *cut* when Billie Holiday sings, "Hush now, don't explain/ Just say you'll remain/ I'm glad you're back/ Don't explain/ Quiet, don't explain / What is there to gain /Skip that lipstick/ Don't explain."
17 Toni Morrison Papers, Box 50 Folder 1–5; Manuscripts Division, Department of Rare Books and Special Collections, Princeton University Library.
18 https://www.nobelprize.org/prizes/literature/1993/morrison/lecture/
19 Faith Ringgold, *We Flew Over the Bridge: The Memoirs of Faith Ringgold* (Durham: Duke University Press, 2005), 162.

20 Jacques Lacan, *The Four Fundamental Concepts of Psychoanalysis*, trans. Alan Sheridan (New York; Norton: 1981 [1973]), 106.
21 https://www.nytimes.com/2015/04/19/books/review/toni-morrisons-god-help-the-child.html
22 Eric Shouse, "Feeling, Emotion, Affect," *M/C Journal* 8.6 (2005). http://journal.media-culture.org.au/0512/03-shouse.php

2
Mood Books

Toni Morrison's move to the production of black blush, in *God Help the Child*, is a part of a long legacy of mood work in African American literature. Langston Hughes' *Ask Your Mama: Twelve Moods for Jazz* (1962) and *In Our Terribleness* (1970), with prose poetry by Amiri Baraka and photography by Fundi (Billy Abernathy), are signature black mood books. The emphasis on "mood," in both of these foundational black avant-garde texts, allows Hughes and Baraka to meet in the space of black feeling. Hughes' subtitle "twelve moods for jazz" shows how deeply he was thinking about the textual production of mood. The experimental form of *Ask Your Mama* is an experiment in ways of making a book gain the texture of feeling (as the reading experience is framed as a "feeling" experience). *In Our Terribleness* is also a textual production of mood. Baraka and Abernathy aim to make readers enter into the mood of "terribleness."

Both Hughes and Baraka were calling for a new type of book which expresses the aspects of black aesthetics that are too abstract to be experienced outside of feeling. Abstraction, in *Ask Your Mama* and *In Our Terribleness*, becomes that space where we confront the limits of explanation, the space where feeling becomes the only way of knowing. When the desire to express feeling makes Hughes and Baraka work the "black book" for its most multi-sensory possibilities, the practice of black abstraction takes over the practice

---

What is African American Literature?, First Edition. Margo N. Crawford.
© 2021 John Wiley & Sons, Inc. Published 2021 by John Wiley & Sons, Inc.

of representing blackness. The difference between the practice of representing blackness and the practice of black abstraction is the difference between explaining blackness and feeling blackness.

Ask Your Mama becomes most abstract when Hughes repeatedly uses the word "tacit" in the marginal notes that are meant to be the musical counterpart of the words on the left hand (proper) side of the page. The musical meaning of "tacet" might matter as much to Hughes as the non-musical meaning of "tacit." The musical term means a pause (a silent interlude). The non-musical term means "expressed or carried on without words or speech" and "implied or indicated (as by an act or by silence) but not actually expressed."[1] Hughes needs both of these meanings as he shapes *Ask Your Mama* around the mood of feeling and not explaining. As "tacit" becomes a refrain in the marginal musical notes, we are forced to pause and hear the lyricism in the musical notes as the two sides of the page begin to become a multidirectional flow of reading. Hughes' call for the tacit is a practice of black abstraction in the sense of these pauses becoming the space where black feeling is experienced in a manner that is too abstract for any words that do not cling to the tacit. Hughes knows that some words do have this ability to not express but gesture toward a feeling.

Hughes and Baraka meet in this zone where there is freedom to be discovered in the tacit (in exchanges of feeling that would stop being felt if they were expressed directly). In *In Our Terribleness*, when Baraka confesses, "I can't say more than that except all the visions and thoughts you've had actually exist," he meets Hughes in this mood of tacit understanding.[2] The experimentalism in *Ask Your Mama* and *In Our Terribleness* is an attempt to feel the rawest, most vulnerable type of tacit black collective feeling. When we let these texts meet in the space of the tacit, we discover Hughes and Baraka's desire to create "mood books," books that take us to a deeper understanding of African American literary tradition as a hailing of those who want to feel the vibrations of blackness (what Baraka, in *In Our Terribleness*, calls "delicate vibratories of ecstatic madness shimmering"). When we read *Ask Your Mama* and *In Our*

Terribleness alongside each other, as a part of a collective feeling (also known as the tradition of African American literature), we feel the wondrously ephemeral but intense connections that create a tradition of "shimmering" and vibrating.

Hughes' Signifying on Signifying

Hughes' refrain "Ask Your Mama" has a tacit quality to it. Hughes uses the classic signifying words "Ask your Mama" as a way of conveying frustration and exhaustion. These title words carry the tacit within them. As opposed to Henry Louis Gates' classic theory of the African American literary tradition as an intertextuality comparable to the vernacular signifying in the dozens, *In Our Terribleness* does not "signify" upon *Ask Your Mama*; the books are a part of an experimental black literature tradition that makes tradition a wobbly, broken affair. The books meet in the break of tradition where there is a tacit understanding that intertextuality cannot fully define whatever African American is and will be.

Throughout *Ask Your Mama*, Hughes makes his refrain "Ask Your Mama" a practice of black abstraction as the black mood that clings to this retort becomes more important than the message the words are trying to convey. The words sound black (to anyone who knows the black signifying tradition), but what makes this retort sound black is more than the signifying tradition. Something too abstract to be explained by tradition is the blackness performed when Hughes gives these words a tacit texture. Hughes' practice of black abstraction becomes the creation of a black mood that hovers around the abstraction (the words themselves). As Hughes signifies on the signifying tradition, he refuses to let these words "Ask Your Mama" feel black only because they are so familiar in black vernacular culture. Hughes makes the words strange and lets us hear the black eccentricity embedded in the African American signifying tradition. Hughes' impulse to create a black mood of eccentricity is what we lose when we think we can explain *Ask Your Mama* (as opposed to simply feeling its movement through moods).

The black eccentric emerges in *Ask Your Mama* as the black traditional emerges. The "lonely flute call" and the "old-time traditional 12-bar blues" is the opening sound.[3] The first words "IN THE/ IN THE QUARTER/ IN THE QUARTER OF THE NEGROES" are a slow sounding out of the full phrase. The speaker composes the phrase as he talks. He finds the longer sequence after testing the sound of the shorter units. When he delivers the full sequence, he has found a way to situate the "quarter." The familiar words "slave quarters" hover over but do not fully capture the more open and clumsy words "of the negroes." Hughes makes these four syllables sound so much less fluid than the four syllables ("in the quarter') that precede them. What might the quarter be, before it settles into a recognizable space? This seems to be Hughes' question as he creates the first "mood" in *Ask Your Mama*'s twelve-mood sequence. The words "IN THE QUARTER OF THE NEGROES" are repeated throughout all twelve moods (all twelve poems). Hughes repeats these words just as he repeats the title words "Ask Your Mama." These two mantras of the text matter. "In the quarter of the negroes" reminds readers, throughout the text, that what has been located (as blackness) has always been such a profound experience of dislocation. The clumsy stumble through those final syllables "of the negroes" makes readers feel the fact that blackness is elsewhere (not in the spaces that have been assigned to African Americans within racial segregation).

The other mantra "Ask Your Mama" makes readers feel the poet's refusal to make this book an answer to any potential question about black aesthetics. Hughes includes the question "Does it [blackness] rub off?" but the "Ask Your Mama" retort has a larger resonance. Any reader wondering how to read this book, how to make sense of the experimental form, or how this book can be so cross-cultural and, also, black is given the answer, "Ask Your Mama." Hughes' foregrounding of mood adds another dimension to his refusal to make the black vernacular signifying tradition the only way to understand his use of the familiar "Ask your mama" phrase. The mood of "Ask Your Mama" gains more nuance when it is not simply a way of shutting down whatever one's interlocutor has said. When Hughes makes "Ask Your Mama" gain the mood of the opaque words of the black eccentric, it becomes clear that, when we treat signifying as the familiar black vernacular tradition, we cannot grasp the more subtle passing on of moods and feelings that makes "literary tradition" sound too stable and intentional. The voice of the black eccentric emerges, subtly, as the signifying in *Ask Your Mama* gains the texture of a person who is trying to find that space to be stylistically unbounded without being "poetically unhep" (Hughes' words in the Liner Notes). In the first mood, Hughes writes, "BY THE RIVER AND THE RAILROAD/ WITH FLUID FAR-OFF GOING/BOUNDARIES BIND UNBINDING" (4). This language "boundaries bind unbinding" shows Hughes' desire, in *Ask Your Mama*, to break out of a binary logic that assumes the unbound does not shape the bound. Unbound blackness (blackness that is not legible) shapes the bound blackness in *Ask Your Mama* (the blackness that announces itself and the blackness that is easily recognizable as the driving force of African American literature). The words "boundaries bind unbinding" suggest the simultaneity of the binding and the unbinding.

Hughes revels in his own entanglement in this binding and unbinding blackness when he, in the first mood, writes, "COME WHAT MAY LANGSTON HUGHES/ IN THE QUARTER OF THE NEGROES/ WHERE THE RAILROAD AND THE RIVER/ HAVE DOORS THAT FACE EACH WAY" (5). Hughes playfully thinks about his own location in the "quarter." In these lines, the quarter is given the railroad tracks and the water that let people in and out. The image of doors facing "each way" adds new dimensions to the feeling of being bound and unbound, simultaneously. "Langston Hughes in the quarter" is within a space that can always be entered and left. The door, the blackness that binds and unbinds, swings both ways; the contours of the "quarter of the negroes" are shaped by this steady movement in and out. What sounds like a dismally segregated space is also, for the speaker of *Ask Your Mama*, a joyously open space.

The poetics of segregated space, in *Ask Your Mama*, does not sound different from the poetics of cross-cultural space. "Langston Hughes in the quarter of the negroes" writes a book that "faces each way." This notion of a book that "faces each way" (like Hughes' image of the doors of railroads and rivers) helps us understand how *Ask Your Mama* exists within the "quarters" we call "African American literature." *Ask Your Mama* teaches us how to feel the difference between the category "African American literature" and the idea of African American literature. Like Michael Gillespie's emphasis on the "idea" of black film, Hughes takes us to the "idea" of black literature. Hughes' emphasis on mood opens up the possibility that black literature is a mood that can never settle into an object of study.[4] The "quarters of blackness" is an idea, not the actual locations that racial segregation created. Hughes, in *Ask Your Mama*, lets himself enter fully into the idea of "LANGSTON HUGHES/ IN THE QUARTER OF THE NEGROES."

As the twelve moods progress, Hughes depicts the idea of African American literature by referring to other black writers (George Schuyler, Ralph Ellison, Arna Bontemps) who make the idea of African American literature something we can feel even if we do not know how exactly these writers come together in the "quarters" of African American literature. Hughes cites these writers not to consolidate a tradition but to feel the mood of a jam session. Calling their names helps him locate himself in the quarter. Calling their names helps him believe that there is some comradeship he can discover through his art. The idea of African American literature is given form when and only when someone feels that there might be some integrity to the idea, some integrity to the feeling (even if there is no formal and essential difference between African American literature and American literature). Hughes finds this feeling in *Ask Your Mama*.

Bodily Feeling in *In Our Terribleness* and *Ask Your Mama*

Baraka seizes this feeling in *In Our Terribleness*. Baraka and Abernathy create a generative tension between the title and the subtitle "Some elements and meaning in black style." The full title connects mood and style. Baraka's words and Abernathy's photographs shape mood into style. "Terribleness" is a mood that Baraka connects to the lived experience of blackness. This lived experience of terribleness is depicted, by Baraka's words and Abernathy's photography, as both an intensely individual experience and a collective experience. The collective nature of this mood (this terribleness) is the part that Baraka and Abernathy want to imagine as "black style." How does mood reorient our understanding of style so that the aesthetic experience cannot be separated from embodiment? *In Our Terribleness* makes writing from the body mean writing from a collective bodily mood, a bodily feeling. Baraka, in *In Our Terribleness*, steadily depicts this bodily feeling in a manner that makes phenomenology of the body deepen into a phenomenology of mood. In "The Phenomenology of Mood and the Meaning of Life," Matthew Ratcliffe develops a lucid theory of the "phenomenology of mood." He convincingly argues that the view that emotions and moods can be "physiological changes that may or may not be experienced" is faulty. He calls for a way of understanding experience that does not create a sharp divide between the intentional and the pre-intentional, the voluntary and the involuntary. This is the very rethinking that Baraka does when he imagines a "black style" that is a collective experience of a "black mood." Baraka uses images of physiological states such as tight muscles to express the intentional and the voluntary. He writes, "It [the communal]" must be represented to our consciousness again, so that it is tight as a supportive muscle must be" (n.p.). Why does Baraka want to make the physiological and the voluntary merge? We can rush to a simple critique of his racial (bodily) essentialism or we can consider his desire (and the larger 1960s and 70s Black Arts Movement desire) to make black body equal black mind. This fundamental undoing of the antiblack separation of black body from mind led the Black Arts Movement to an investment in bodily feeling as a means of decolonizing the mind.

In Our Terribleness performs this decolonizing of the mind through the Black Power embrace of bodily feeling. Hughes and Baraka both develop a poetics of bodily mood. Hughes' use of the word "figurine" in the book's marginal literary soundtrack makes bodily feeling become the aura of each use of the "Ask Your Mama" refrain. In the opening page of the text, Hughes explains, "The musical figurine indicated after each 'Ask your mama' line may incorporate the impudent little melody of the old break, 'Shave and a haircut, fifteen cents'" (n.p.). In the marginal soundtrack notes, Hughes never uses the full phrase "musical figurine." He simply writes, "figurine." The common meaning of this word is "a statuette, especially one of a human form." Hughes makes this word "figurine" express what the refrain "Ask Your Mama" is supposed to make readers feel. In other parts of the marginal soundtrack notes, Hughes explains the instruments, sounds, and songs that should shape the mood of the words in the text proper. Hughes' use of word "figurine" gestures to a musical mood that he cannot express by referring to particular instruments. The non-musical meaning of "figurine" (a representation of a human form) shifts the marginal soundtrack notes from music to bodily feeling.

Hughes' use of "figurine" gives the book another dimension, the explicit emphasis on black mood as a bodily environment. Unlike *In Our Terribleness*, *Ask Your Mama* does not celebrate the black body; as he celebrates black music, he lets images of the black body merge into the background of the musical environment of the book. His prime image of the "Ask your Mama" signifying is a play with the racist children-like questioning of whether or not darker skin color "rubs off." Hughes refuses to let the black-body-in-pain overdetermine the musical environment that the book becomes. He writes, "AND THEY ASKED ME RIGHT AT CHRISTMAS/ IF MY BLACKNESS, WOULD IT RUB OFF?/ I SAID, ASK YOUR MAMA" (8). Maurice

Merleau-Ponty theorizes the body-in-an-environment in the following manner: "The body is the vehicle of being in the world, and having a body is, for a living creature, to be intervolved with a definite environment, to identify oneself with certain projects and be continually committed to them."[5] This "intervolving" (the rolling that makes it impossible to separate body from environment) is the reason why a phenomenology of black bodily feeling (or bodily mood) differs from a phenomenology of the black body. The multimedia quality of *Ask Your Mama* and *In Our Terribleness* makes these books feel like a multisensory environment.

Both Hughes and Baraka stage the difference between the black bodily mood that is "intervolved" with a dynamic environment and the naturalized images of the black body that is always already marked by the insidious antiblack gaze. Hughes stages this difference in the fourth mood, "Ode to Dinah," when he writes, "IN THE SHADOW OF THE QUARTER/ WHERE THE PEOPLE ALL ARE DARKER/ NOBODY NEEDS A MARKER./ AMEN IS NOT AN ENDING/ BUT JUST A PUNCTUATION" (31). In this sequence, Hughes begins with the phenomenology of the black body and then slides, with the words "AMEN IS NOT AN ENDING," into the phenomenology of black mood. Baraka's use of "Amen," in *In Our Terribleness*, makes "Amen" a bodily mood that differs greatly from the language of static black embodiment conveyed by words like "WHERE THE PEOPLE ALL ARE DARKER." Like Hughes, Baraka makes "Amen" signal the turn to black mood. Baraka writes, "like the bloods say A-a-Men …A-a-Men … A-a-Men …A-Men, A-Men, thinking bout home." Like Hughes' working of words for their most sonic possibilities, Baraka stretches out "Amen" as he tries to make readers feel the sound as a mood that is "bout home." When Hughes insists that the word is "punctuation," and "not an ending," he conveys the idea that "Amen" can, like a period mark, express a shift and pause. As Hughes moves from the phenomenology of the black body to the phenomenology of black mood, he implies with the words

"AMEN IS NOT AN ENDING" that the difference between the black body discourse and the black mood discourse is the totalizing effect of the "black body" (a narrative with a beginning and ending that becomes the effect of antiblack racism). As Hughes and Baraka trouble the "black body in the antiblack gaze" discourse, they signal (through these uses of "Amen") the "writing from black mood" that is more subtle and unfixable than "writing from the body."

The beginning of the eleventh mood "Jazztet Muted" is another key passage, in *Ask Your Mama*, that stages this tension between the phenomenology of the black body and the phenomenology of black mood. Hughes writes:

> IN THE NEGROES OF THE QUARTER
> PRESSURE OF THE BLOOD IS SLIGHTLY HIGHER IN THE QUARTER OF THE NEGROES WHERE BLACK SHADOWS MOVE LIKE SHADOWS
> CUT FROM SHADOWS CUT FROM SHADE
> IN THE QUARTER OF THE NEGROES
> SUDDENLY CATCHING FIRE
> FROM THE WING TIP OF A MATCH TIP
> ON THE BREATH OF ORNETTE COLEMAN. (77)

The move from "facts" of the black body (high blood pressure) to the shadows and other images of evanescence allows Hughes, in this sequence, to revel in a jazz mood of improvisation. The fact of high blood pressure is not as meaningful to Hughes as the pressure to improvise created by the jazz mood. In this sequence, Hughes overshadows the reference to the black body with the image of shadows. Fanon's iconic formulation "a slow composition of my self as a body in the middle of a spatial and temporal world" is reshaped by Hughes into the mood of "a slow composition of my shadow as a self in the middle of a spatial and temporal world."[6] Hughes moves from the realism of the high blood pressure to the abstraction of the shadows as he suggests that any phenomenology of the black body (as opposed to a phenomenology of black mood) will fail to understand that black subjects never lose the excessiveness and uncontainability of mood and vibrations even as they are, as Baraka explains in *In Our Terribleness*, "trapped in screens of negative description" (36).

Baraka makes the tension between phenomenology of mood and phenomenology of body as pronounced as it is in *Ask Your Mama*. The passages in *In Our Terribleness* that depict the black collective body differ greatly from the passages that revel in the collective mood of "terribleness." The passages that are most directly tied to the Black Arts Movement nationalist discourse of the collective black body are:

So we are parts of a body. And this is what you see. The energy revealed. [...] From the kids the simbas to the old folks, sweet sisters in between, what will hold us in motion, [...] (133)

And all of us are one body, man. Dig it? One body. As each is a small, as each of our organs is a small, and we, the large, so the nation, is the large in relationship to us. (136)

The path of the peoples.
The Whole Body:

Children
Dudes
Bloods
Sisters
Old People (Ol Folks)
Roots (102)

These passages appear after many pages of words and photographs that let readers feel "terribleness" as a black mood that does not settle into a black collective body. Baraka depicts the mood of terribleness as a form of black affect that is too personal and "black" to settle into the collective black body that the book hails. Terribleness is, in many passages in *In Our Terribleness*, a collective feeling incredibly tied to a black individuality that he explains, in his 1964 play *The Slave*, in the following manner: "But listen now... Brown is not brown except when used as an intimate description of personal phenomenological fields. As your brown is not my brown, et cetera, that is, we need, ahem, a meta-language. We need some thing not included here. [Spreads arms]."[7] In *In Our Terribleness*, Baraka extends this explicit focus on phenomenology. Baraka depicts mood (terribleness) as environment: "All our terribleness is our total" (71). Terribleness is also given the quality of a collective nervous system: "tight as a supportive muscle must be" (118). These images show Baraka pushing against the other passages that make it impossible to remember that the "fact" of a "black body" is the idea of a black body. With these images of black mood as an environment and a collective nervous system, Baraka, like Hughes, reconsiders black bodily feeling as a literary mood that flows deeper than the "writing from the body," shared styles, deformation of mastery, signifying, or shared themes that have been viewed as the specificity of black literary traditions.

Rethinking Literary Tradition Through Mood

In one of his most widely anthologized poems "The Negro Speaks of Rivers," Hughes writes, "I've known rivers.../ I've known rivers ancient as the world and older than the flow/ of human blood in human veins./ My soul has grown deep like the rivers."[8] This Harlem Renaissance-era poem is one of Hughes' most familiar sonic flows and yet we have not felt the bodily mood that these lines emphasize. Hughes makes the river flow, blood flow, and soul flow converge. The line "My soul has grown deep like the rivers" anticipates all of the ways that "soul," during the Black Arts Movement, becomes a mood that defines blackness. Hughes, in this poem, like *Ask Your Mama*, is writing from a space where bodily feeling is the meaning of heritage and tradition. Mood books, like *Ask Your Mama* and *In Our Terribleness*, offer a new way of understanding how black literary aesthetics (on the lower frequencies famously hailed by Ellison) becomes a mood. Writers who feel the spell of this mood create whatever differentiates African American literature from other literary traditions. Writing from black mood is writing in charged air; writing from black embodiment seems like an attempt to chain air. Baraka, in *In Our Terribleness*, describes the black mood that resists this chained air. He insists, "I can unchain air held to a stone be myself gettin up!" (n.p.).

In *Ask Your Mama*, Hughes, of course, makes "mood" his explicit approach to black aesthetics. This book, framed so directly as a mood book, performs writing from black mood as the working of words for their most sonic possibilities. Sound is mood, for Hughes, but *Ask Your Mama* makes sound hard to hear, at times, and easier to feel as a potentiality, as a performance that we are still waiting to experience. The overall mood of *Ask Your Mama* may be anticipation. Anticipation is given a texture of blackness in *Ask Your Mama*. "When the Saints Come Marchin In" cannot be contained by the marginal soundtrack notes. The song spills out to the other side of the page and throughout the entire book. The joy in this song is a joy inspired by sheer hope ("Lord I want to be in that number"). The joy is the feeling that "I" really could be in that "number." The song delivers the wonder of that possibility that is anticipated in such a visceral manner. The singers are feeling, deeply, what is not yet here.

The lingering mood of *In Our Terribleness* is also anticipation. Baraka's mood work of anticipation gains a crucial new dimension when he announces, "The buildings will be attitudes, vibrating like James Brown the ecstasy of the ultimate" (n.p.). The following passage appears before this anticipation of the attitudinal architecture:

> Dude with the pointing finger. […] He cd be saying, arguing Fanon or w/DebilMoon about how/ we gonna finally take over our own space in these same shitty/ towns transforming them with our vision and style to be extensions/ of swiftshake and stomp sound. (n.p.)

Just as the buildings will be attitudes, the book, *In Our Terribleness*, is an attitude. Baraka is anticipating a mood architecture that reshapes urban space and literary space around the energy of "swiftshake and stomp sound." The idea that the buildings and books can be "extensions" of "swiftshake and stomp sound" suggests that the energy of this sonic everyday black movement can be rechanneled into the structure of buildings and books. The Empire State Building is described, in *In Our Terribleness*, as "white feeling" (136). The mood architecture of black feeling is what Baraka and Abernathy aim to produce as they very deliberately construct a "black book." In a 1969 letter to Baraka (with poster-style graphics), Abernathy reminds Baraka, his collaborator, that they must complete their "black book" mission:

> Our BLACK BOOK WILL BE THE WORLD'S GREATEST CREATION
> FOR BLACKNESS MIND MIRROR MAGIC
> the Hypnotic force of BLACK LOVE will conquer UGLINESS AND endure[9]

Abernathy's idea of the "Black book" was overdetermined by the Black Arts Movement desire to create textual space that was not affected by the space and energy of the dominant aesthetic that Baraka calls "white feeling."

What are the contours of black feeling? How do *In Our Terribleness* and *Ask Your Mama* perform both a binding and unbinding of black feeling? The textual production of black feeling, in these books, is an experiment in making a book feel unbound in spite of the literal binding that makes the pages a book. Baraka and Hughes create two deeply experimental texts that are experiments in creating the feeling of black mood as the unbound. Hughes conjures up the aura of the unbound by making the book seem like a record. His liner notes, at the end of the text, signal this desire to make a book feel like a phonograph. But the liner notes also function as narrative counterparts to the poems in the text proper. We finish the book needing to put the needle on the record and hear these poems again as we try to figure out what to do with the cryptic liner notes that only convince us that Hughes does not want his lyricism to be decoded. *In Our Terribleness* also ends with the note

Mood Books

of the unbound. The last words are "Then get your hat i.e., get up and go" (160). Throughout the entire book, Baraka continues to pause at key moments and sign his name before the text resumes. The pauses and multiple endings that become beginnings perform a mood of melancholy and ecstasy as Baraka imagines that he is a hypnotist trying to guide his readers to their own self-hypnotism. One performance of the pause reads, "Here the contact is broken," and is followed by Baraka's signature. The signing of the name becomes a part of the text, not a part of the paratext in the manner of the nineteenth century slave narratives that used the signature as a way of proving that the narrative was actually written by the enslaved African. When Baraka makes the signature a part of the art of the text itself, he may be pushing against the white publishing industry that begins its framing of black texts with the slave narratives. Baraka, with his signing of his name throughout the text, may be asserting the new form of the self-authenticating black interiority that the Black Arts Movement embraced.

Hughes' last book *Black Misery* (1969) is not a "black mood book" in the manner of *Ask Your Mama* and *In Our Terribleness*. *Black Misery* begs to be compared to *In Our Terribleness*. The "black misery" differs greatly from the "terribleness." Hughes was asked to write a black version of the *Misery* children's books written by Suzanne Heller. These mid-1960s humorous children's books, illustrated by line drawings, attracted a wide audience and the publisher decided to produce a "black" counterpart. Hughes died before he completed *Black Misery*, but the publisher decided that Hughes had written enough to warrant publishing the book as a complete text. *Black Misery* is a word and image text, with Hughes' words and black and white drawings by Arouni (Lynette Logan). Hughes follows the model of Heller and writes a string of examples of misery: "Misery is when you heard on the radio that the neighborhood you live in is a slum but you always thought it was home. [...] Misery is when you can see all the other kids in the dark but they claim they can't see you. [...] Misery is when you first realize so many things bad have black in them, like black cats, black arts, blackball."[10] The tone of the book is pure melancholy; there is no trace of *Ask Your Mama*'s impudence and refusal to make blackness something that is explained as opposed to felt.

We might wonder why did Hughes write this book that has no connection to *Ask Your Mama*'s mood of black interiority and black opaqueness. The refrain "Ask Your Mama" delivers a bodacious joy that refuses the marketing of misery as black. Suzanne Heller's *Misery* children's book series included three titles – *Misery* (1964), *More Misery* (1965), and *Misery Loves Company* (1967). As opposed to Hughes' shaping of *Ask Your Mama* around "twelve moods," Hughes' *Black Misery* presents the monotony of one mood – the black child's misery as intentional and unintentional racism continues to overdetermine the black child's everyday life. *Black Misery* lacks the "joy of living and the stretching of the social elastic" that Hughes describes in the liner notes for the tenth mood "Bird in Orbit" (91). This tenth mood ends with the marginal soundtrack note of "Flute call into very far-out boopish blues" (74). *Black Misery* makes the blues lose its "boopishness." *Ask Your Mama* and *In Our Terribleness* express the "very far-out boopish blues" that lets black feeling remain too "far out" to settle into the quick and easy narratives in *Black Misery*.

Hughes may have viewed the publisher's desire to market "Black Misery" as absurd. He may have viewed each explanation of misery, in this children's book, as an expression of his own misery working within a white-dominated publishing industry that cannot envision horizons past this "black misery" and naturalizes what Jennifer Nash refers to as an "archive of pain." Like Baraka and Abernathy's opening mirror page in *In Our Terribleness* (a full-page silver page that allows the black ideal readers to see their own face as they enter into the book), Hughes may have dreamt of a paratext for *Black Misery* that would shatter the framing of blackness as always already other. After Hughes' death in 1967, *Black Misery* was published, in 1969, a year before the publication of *In Our Terribleness*. We might wonder how Hughes would have felt as he read *In Our Terribleness* and entered into its performance of the black book as a black mirror. *In Our Terribleness* may have convinced Hughes that Baraka ("that boy LeRoi," as Hughes called him) was indeed, as Carl Van Vechten wrote in a 1964 letter to Hughes, one of the latest wave of "new negroes" who would take the ongoing black cultural renaissance to a new level of freedom. Van Vechten writes:

> Dear Langston, You and I have been through so many new negroes that we are a little tired of it all. BUT I was really excited about the group you have brought together. Le Roi Jones who appears to be somebody [...]."[11]

In the 1960s and early 1970s, Langston Hughes and Amiri Baraka (LeRoi Jones) were both interested in mood as a way of understanding black aesthetics. *Ask Your Mama* and *In Our Terribleness* are black mood books written at the beginning and end of a decade that Hughes describes, in "The Task of the Negro Writer as Artist" (1965), as "the decade of a tremendous freedom movement in which all of us can take pride."[12] While Hughes was completing *Black Misery*, during the height of the Black Power movement, he may have been anticipating a discourse that would make the words "black misery" an oxymoron. Baraka's Black Power imaging of terribleness mobilized blackness as too terrible to be miserable. Hughes' dedication of the liner notes in *Ask Your Mama* – "for the poetically unhep" – gains a new meaning when applied to *In Our Terribleness*. Only the poetically "hep," those who feel this terribleness, will understand that this terribleness does not mean black misery.

Notes

1 "Tacit." *Merriam-Webster.com*. Merriam-Webster, n.d. Web. 9 Sept 2018.
2 Amiri Baraka and Fundi (Billy Abernathy), *In Our Terribleness: Some Elements and Meaning in Black Style* (Indianapolis: Bobbs-Merrill Co., 1970), n.p.

What is African American Literature?

3 Langston Hughes, *Ask Your Mama: 12 Moods for Jazz* (New York: Knopf, 1961), 3, 4.
4 Michael Boyce Gillespie, *Film Blackness: American Cinema and the Idea of Black Film* (Durham : Duke University, 2016).
5 Maurice Merleau-Ponty, *Phenomenology of Perception*, trans. Colin Smith. (London and New York: Routledge, 2002 [1945]), 82.
6 Frantz Fanon, *Black Skins, White Masks*, trans. Charles Markmann (New York: Grove Press, 1967), 111.
7 Amiri Baraka, *Dutchman and the Slave* (New York: Perennial, 2001 [1964]), 45.
8 Langston Hughes, "The Negro Speaks of Rivers" in *The New Negro: Voices of the Harlem Renaissance* (New York: Touchstone, 1997 [1925], 141.
9 Fundi Abernathy to Amiri Baraka, 5 May 1969, Amiri Baraka Papers, box 12, Moorland Spingarn Research Center, Howard University.
10 Langston Hughes, *Black Misery* (New York and Oxford: Oxford University Press, 1994 [1969]), n. p.
11 Emily Barnard, ed. *Remember Me to Harlem: the Letters of Langston Hughes and Carl Van Vechten, 1925–1964* (New York: Knopf, 2001), 323.
12 Faith Berry, ed. *Good Morning Revolution: Uncollected Writings of Langston Hughes* (New York: Citadel Press, 1992 [1973]), 171.

3
The Vibrations of African American Literature

[…] More concerned with the vibrations of the Word, than with the Word itself.

—Larry Neal[1]

[T]he object vibrates against its frame like a resonator, and troubled air gets out.

—Fred Moten[2]

How does the *is-ness* of African American literature become the shared atmosphere of vibrations? The is-ness vibrates against the frame "African American literature"; the is-ness is the "troubled air" (Moten 182). The moments of unapologetic lyricism for the sake of escape from narrative are the moments when we feel the is-ness of African American literature most acutely.

As Stephen Henderson, in *Understanding the New Black Poetry* (1972), proposed that "saturation" (saturated blackness) was the distinctive quality of African American poetry, he framed his understanding of the is-ness of African American poetry as the "Soul" that cannot be understood if it is analyzed as an abstraction. His emphasis on the need to "experience" the saturated blackness leads him to the image of reading as immersion. He writes, "[T]he recognition of Blackness in poetry […] must rest upon one's immersion in

What is African American Literature?, First Edition. Margo N. Crawford.
© 2021 John Wiley & Sons, Inc. Published 2021 by John Wiley & Sons, Inc.

the totality of the Black Experience."[3] But Henderson defies his own theory of reading as immersion when he gestures toward his inability to fully explain saturation. As he emerges from the all-knowingness of immersion to what cannot be explained, he uses the idea of infinity and "Soul" as his only way of gesturing to the is-ness of African American poetry. In the midst of Henderson's attempt to create a narrative of the emergence of black poetry, the lyricism of infinity echoes when Henderson channels Amiri Baraka's poem "Black Art" as he muses, "Black People are poems" (68). Henderson's lyrical eruption allows readers to *feel*, for a fleeting moment, the saturation that cannot be felt in his narrative analysis.

Henderson's theory of saturated blackness as the distinguishing feature of African American poetry breaks apart into the feeling of vibration when he imagines the "Soul-Field." He writes:

> And when I say Soul-Field, I have in mind an analogy to a magnetic field or to a gravitational field, at the center of which would be that unique cluster of forces, events, personalities, and sensibility that have created that complexity that we casually call the Black Experience. Some parts of it are denser than others [...]
> (74-75)

When the is-ness of African American literature is approached through the textual production of black feeling, the "dense" parts of the Soul-Field of the literature are the most magnetic energies with the most vibration. The faster moving prose versus the state of lyrical suspension is a change in the pitch of African American literature. From the very beginning of African American literature, there has been a tension between a narrative that authenticates African American literature and a lyrical, vibratory impulse that cannot be contained by any narrative explanation of what African American literature is. When Henderson stops interpreting the black saturation, he moves from hermeneutics to the felt experience of poetics (the only way of accessing the is-ness of African American literature).[4]

The Vibrations of African American Literature

When Phillis Wheatley was put on trial as the white dignitaries were asked to judge her ability to write poetry, the tension between the felt experience of the black lyrical impulse and the racial narrative of the white racist patriarchs was on display. Wheatley's poetry has continued to vibrate in spite of a discourse of white racist patriarchy that could not feel the vibratory power of the poesis of black girlhood. When we re-read Wheatley as a poet of black girlhood, what *vibrates* in her poems differs greatly from the anti-black, racist framing narratives such as "written by Phillis, a young Negro Girl, who was but a few Years since, brought an uncultivated Barbarian from Africa." We gain a different sense of the archive of feeling in African American literature when we imagine Wheatley, the young enslaved girl, absorbing the pain in words she heard or read that justified slavery through the rhetoric of white saviors. Wheatley's repetition of words (such as "Twas mercy brought me from my Pagan land/ Taught my benighted soul to understand") signals much more than regurgitation.[5] The words re-sound and make us feel the limits of the anti-black discourse young Wheatley has swallowed. We feel a pain that cannot be reduced to a slave's imitation of the master discourse. On the deepest registers, we feel the vibration of the master discourse through the nerve endings of a young enslaved African girl.

African American literature is an archive of feelings that allows Wheatley's vibrations to remain too electric and opaque to be fully understood outside of her most private emotional journey. "Twas mercy" lingers as Wheatley's right to feel mercy in any manner that allows her to feel that her writing is her resumption. The feeling of resumption as redemption is given form in the public art sculpture of Wheatley in Boston. Wheatley appears to be sitting and, also, ready to stand up. The folds in her dress are wavy as the vibrations of her words "twas mercy" that do not make sense unless we allow these words to be as unsettled as she appears in the Boston public memorial.

Alexis Pauline Gumbs, in M Archive: After the End of the World, imagines Wheatley's breath changing after her Middle Passage. Gumbs writes, "knots in her chest ever tightened. her own breath forever linked to the oxygen tank of western inspiration."[6] Gumbs

What is African American Literature?

Figure 5. Author's Photograph. Boston, Massachusetts.

imagines another "tank of inspiration" as she moves from the images of Wheatley's loss of the ability to breath freely to the image of black collective aesthetic movement— "here the only movement is us" (131). These words "here the only movement is us" capture the is-ness of African American literature that is the individuality of writers and a state of collective becoming. The is-ness of African American literature is the *incredible* movement of us (not any type of easy or inevitable movement). Like the vibration of a pendulum, the individuality of the writers coexists with a state of "us" (as opposed to a linear movement from individuality to the collective).

In the literary cookbook *Vibration Cooking: or the Travel Notes of a Geechee Girl* (1970), Vertamae Grosvenor makes vibration a way of cooking and, also, a way of thinking about blackness as a structure of feeling. Throughout this cookbook mix of recipes and narratives, the lyrical emerges as the vibration that defies any formula or recipe. *Vibration Cooking* reveals the tension between the order of narrative and the contingency of the lyrical. Victor Hernandez Cruz, in the poetic afterword of *Vibration Cooking*, writes, "but here we all are/ in vertas [sic] soul space kitchen/ taking off."[7] *Vibration Cooking* teaches us to read the is-ness of African American literature as the "soul space kitchen/ taking off" (n.p.). With the mix of spaceship energy and the homespun, Grosvenor performs the simultaneity of the flight and the groundedness of black writers whose art is the complex collection and recollection of vibrations. Grosvenor explains, in the beginning of *Vibration Cooking*, that she does not cook by measuring or weighing anything. She writes, "If you have any trouble, I would check out your kitchen vibrations. *What kinds of pots are you using?*" (xiv). Her assemblage of autobiographical stories, letters, recipes, travel narratives, and cultural analysis becomes her practice of vibration.

Toward the end of *Vibration Cooking*, Grosvenor includes a letter to the visual artist Bob Thompson. As she addresses the deceased Bob Thompson, she begins by explaining to Thompson that she attended his memorial service and felt that it lacked the feeling and rhythm that Thompson embodied. She writes, "Waiting for them to get into the rhythm of your lifestyle. Waiting for them to feel" (179). This notion of "waiting for them to feel" underscores that, for Grosvenor, there is need to create space, within appreciations of black art, for the rhythm, the vibrations, that push against the "memorial service" that shuts down feeling.

Feeling of Vibration (Not Imitation)

Phillis Wheatley shows us that, from the very beginning of African American literature, writers were feeling what Fred Moten describes as "troubled air," the vibration of black affect within the enclosure of antiblackness. Wheatley's poetry expresses feelings that are too raw and unfiltered to fit into the narrative of imitation that developed, over the years, as critics assessed her work. When Alice Walker describes Wheatley's poetry as "stiff, struggling, ambivalent," it becomes clear that Walker is opening up a new way of understanding

Wheatley's tense poetics.[8] Walker helps us hear the nervous strain in Wheatley's poetry. As opposed to the assumption that Wheatley's desire to imitate the sounds of whiteness is producing the nervousness and the quivers, Walker wonders if the quivers are better understood as the affect that is "struggling" to be a beginning of African American poetry. Wheatley's tremors are pathologized when critics read her poetry as the stuntedness of imitation. Wheatley's poetic tremors, when not pathologized, gain the ability to vibrate. The shaking in her words can continue to shake when we resist the need to make her be still and firmly situated in any origin narrative of African American poetry as moving from imitation to the freedom and achievement of black sound. The vibration in Wheatley's poetry is the feeling that the stiffness is moving (the feeling that there is a difference between still words and stiff words).

The image of the harp, in Wheatley's poem "On the Death of a Young Gentleman," opens up Alice Walker's non-pathologizing interest in Wheatley's "stiff, struggling, ambivalent" sound (405). The harp creates sound out of vibrations of air. Wheatley's image of the harp, in this poem, has great significance when we consider Wheatley's anticipation of the late eighteenth century poetry influenced by the new technology of the Aeolian harp (the harp played by wind) developed during this era. In "Nerves, Vibration and the Aeolian Harp," Shelley Trower analyzes the late eighteenth-century emergence of the harp as a metaphor for the poet who works with "incoming" and "outgoing" vibrations.[9] In Wheatley's poetry, there are repeated word usages, such as "nerve unstrung," "poetik strains," and "vocal strings," that show that Wheatley subtly approached the idea of "poetry as the Aeolian harp" that Coleridge and other poets more directly depicted in the later years of the eighteenth century. Like a harp placed in a window and played by the wind, when Wheatley's poetry was reduced, by the white dignitaries, to the poetic aspiration of "the African," Wheatley was denied the power to be more than a receptacle of incoming vibrations. When we recognize the many gestures to nerves and strains in her poems, we gain a deeper sense of how she was playing the harp – she was not a harp being played. Wheatley's *outgoing* vibrations may be the moments, in her poems, when a voice that strains vibrates until the strain does not signal the social death of the black subject who has swallowed a discourse that makes her not fully human. When we approach the is-ness of African American literature through affect, outgoing vibrations allow us to rethink the is-ness as what flows out of the category (as the energy that cannot be felt if we are not reading with an eye for what is outgoing and emergent). Wheatley's poetry is too outgoing to be the stable origin of African American poetry. How would we ever figure out the *origin* of outgoing vibrations?

Many of Wheatley's heavy, elegiac poems have moments of lightness (that feel like the harp-like breeze in Romantic poetry that she anticipates). The role of affect in Wheatley's poetry becomes most clear when the lighter breeze emerges with an unformed aura that vibrates against the emotional legibility of the elegiac form. Rowan Ricardo Phillips argues, in *When Blackness Rhymes with Blackness*, that the mystery of Wheatley's poetry is its mix of didacticism and obsequiousness.[10] The push of the didacticism against the obsequiousness produces the sound of what is created between incoming and outgoing vibrations. Imagine the sound of "Twas mercy brought me from my pagan land" splitting into "Twas mercy" and "brought me from my pagan land" and producing the unspeakable sound in between as the outgoing vibration of whatever African American literature becomes when we allow the category to morph into a feeling.

In *When Blackness Rhymes with Blackness*, Phillips muses that Wheatley is infinitely cited but very difficult to quote. As he argues that Wheatley's poetry has functioned as an epigraph that is never brought into the realm of actual analysis, he approaches the idea that we still do not know how to read Wheatley. For Phillips, the epigraphic mood is the feeling that hovers as studies of African American literature continue to privilege narrative and use the lyrical as a means of analyzing narrative. Phillips reminds us that the lyric must be given more attention, if African American literary studies is going to deepen its attention to the nuances of black literary sound. The epigraphic use of poetry (the use of poetry as a pathway into prose) shows a deeper dimension of how approaching African American literature through historicism differs from approaching African American literature through feeling. If we did break out of this use of poetry as epigraph, we would feel the difference between narrative satisfaction and catharsis and lyrical wonder and tremble.

Wheatley keeps trembling in Nikki Giovanni's poem "Linkage (for Phillis Wheatley)." In this poem, as Giovanni revels in the *elsewhere* of ellipsis marks, she discovers the is-ness of African American literature in the elsewhere of the lyrical that escapes narrative. The poem's tension pivots on the final move to the word "elsewheres."[11] Giovanni makes Wheatley signal black literary "elsewheres." The poem performs the tension between the movement of words and the pause created by ellipsis marks. The words remain suspended even as Giovanni tries to create the "linkage" announced by the title. Giovanni writes, "The record sticks. . .Phillis was her own precedent" (27). The notion of a writer not having a precedent sounds remarkably similar to Lucille Clifton's words "won't you celebrate with me/ what i have shaped into/a kind of life? i had no model," in her poem "won't you celebrate with me" (1993). Giovanni makes Wheatley matter not as some type of starting point of a literary tradition but rather as an "elsewhere" that hails many other black women writers who create within the space of elsewhere. In "won't you celebrate with me," Clifton describes this black poetic elsewhere as a bridge: "I made it up/here on this bridge between/ starshine and clay." Giovanni places Wheatley on this bridge where "shared elsewheres" create the tradition of African American women's poetry.

A 1972 conversation between Margaret Walker and Nikki Giovanni reveals the deepest dimensions of Giovanni's *idea* of African American literature. The following exchange occurs:

> Walker: (leaning back in her chair) Well, now you have asked a real aesthetic question and I think a good one. Sometimes a work of art is popular. Rarely is that true because for something to be popular

it must appeal to the taste of the masses, and in many instances the taste of the masses is not what we call a cultivated taste.

Giovanni: (raises voice) But that is NOTHING BUT ARROGANCE!
   [...]
Walker: Well, now you're saying that they don't have to have a cultivated taste?
   Giovanni: I'm saying that art is not for the cultivated taste. It is to cultivate a taste.[12]

Giovanni's words "I'm saying that art is not for the cultivated taste [...] It is to cultivate taste" capture the power of her idea of African American literature. Just as poets such as Whitman innovated poetry itself by cultivating a taste for long lines, Giovanni has innovated black poetry itself by cultivating a taste for the textual production of black feeling. Giovanni's focus on the poetic production of black feeling (as an interaction between poet and reader) is performed in "Kidnap Poem" (1968). She writes:

> ever been kidnapped
> by a poet
> if I were a poet
> i'd kidnap you
> put you in my phrases and meter
> you to jones beach
> or maybe coney island
> or maybe just to my house
> lyric you in lilacs
> dash you in the rain
> blend into the beach
> to complement my see
> play the lyre for you
> ode you with my love song
> anything to win you
> wrap you in the red Black green
> show you off to mama
> yeah if I were a poet i'd kid
> nap you[13]

In order to understand how Giovanni wants the poem to become a shared atmosphere (between poet and reader), we need to lean into words such as "i'd kidnap you/ *put you in* my phrases." This "put you in" dimension of Giovanni's poetics of space matters. She wants readers to co-create the interior of the poems. As her poems stage this tension between being inside and outside a poem, she lets us feel the difference between just reading a poem and being kidnapped by poetics (being brought into an affective atmosphere). When she writes, "meter/ you to jones beach/ or maybe coney island/ or maybe just to my house," her "house" (as in the book *My House*) is the space of feeling, the structure of feeling, that can only be known if we enter into the vibrations of the poetry. The vibrations (the black feelings) matter more than the meter. The vibrations make meter into an action – "*meter/* you to jones beach" (19).

The poetry vibrates because it is activating a collective nervous system, that which Paula Giddings, in her introduction to Giovanni's *Cotton Candy on a Rainy Day* (1978), describes in the following manner:

> Our idiosyncracies, our involuntary reflexes, the imperfect stroke is often the signature of a work because it makes it unique and personal—like a fingerprint:
>
> > but I sit writing
> > a poem
> > about my habits
> > which while it's not
> > a great poem
> > is mine
>
> It is not important to her that her poems live in greatness, but that they live. That they have the force to pull someone in, who may say, 'Yes, I have felt that way. No. I am not alone.' That is their great test. The heart, not the form, is the final arbiter. (14)

Giddings' emphasis on "heart," "not form," should make us rethink Giovanni's practice of form as heart work, as demonstrated in

"Kidnap Poem." To "lyric you in lilacs" and "dash you in the rain" is to deform any understanding of form that cannot feel the *heart work* that is pulling "you" into the "lyric" and the "dash."

In the poem "You Came, Too," Giovanni pulls "you" alongside "I" in a manner that shows how deeply committed Giovanni is to the "kidnap poetics" of pulling readers into a shared atmosphere of feeling. The final lines in the poem are: "I went from the crowd seeking you/ I went from the crowd seeking me/ I went from the crowd forever/ You came, too." The speaker of the poem finds the space to be what Fred Moten calls the "unalone soloist."[14] The heart is the form in this poem. The anaphora dissipates once "I" finds "you." The final words "you came, too" (the final break out of the stanzas) make us feel a tenderness that the form (the anaphora) cannot express. In Giovanni's poem "Adulthood," the young speaker wonders why she did not become a debutante "instead of a for real Black person who must now feel" (70). Giovanni, like this speaker, decides to keep foregrounding feeling as a way of creating a poetics that will pull readers into that which is "for real Black." And this "for real blackness" is expansive. In her poem "Space," we see that this "for real blackness" is a journey into black outer space. Giovanni writes, "i always wanted to know space/ people but how do we proceed" (73). Giovanni is a space-maker. As she turns heart into form, she does indeed remain tied to what Glissant calls the poet's "shock of elsewhere." Her poem "Linkage (for Phillis Wheatley)" includes the word "elsewheres." The poetic shock of elsewhere, in this poem, becomes the final move in the poem to the question of home for Wheatley. Giovanni writes, "What must life be… to any young captive…of its time…Do we send them back…home to the remembered horrors…Do we allow them their elsewheres" (27). Giovanni allows Wheatley her "elsewheres"; she does not try to understand Wheatley's lines, breaks, and cuts. The poem lets us feel that Giovanni, as she explains in her poem "My House," is trying to speak *through* English as the flow and placeholder function of the ellipsis marks begin to signal stranded affect, affect that is looking for a legible form.[15] The title of the poem "Linkage" only makes sense if we see linkage as what is created when Wheatley's elsewhere is pulled into Giovanni's elsewhere. As Paula Giddings insists, for Giovanni, the "heart, not the form, is the final arbiter." Giovanni's impulse to feel Wheatley's elsewhere makes the poem's ellipsis marks the *form* of feeling what cannot be known.

In *Hoodoo Hollerin' Bebop Ghosts*, Larry Neal chants: "O Ancestor faces form on film our minds/ form our contours out of deep wailing saxes./ form in the voice our would-be leaders./ form child./ form in the rush of war./form child./ form in the sun's explosion."[16] In Neal's words "form child," we hear such a tender call for form that is inseparable from feeling. As Kevin Young thinks about form in relation to blues poetry, he asserts, "With the blues, the form fights the feeling."[17] Young thinks about form as trying to contain or re-channel the feeling. Like Neal and Giovanni, Young taps into the central tension of "feeling and form" in African American literature. Giovanni's poetics of feeling teaches us that the feeling can be the form. The feeling as form in Giovanni's poetry is her starting point – the volume *Black Feeling Black Talk* (1968) – and the taste that she continues to "cultivate." When Giovanni expresses black feeling through the reflection on how we cannot know what Wheatley was actually feeling, the title of the poem – "Linkage" – becomes a way of feeling the tradition of African American literature as a linkage of elsewheres (that which Baraka, in *In Our Terribleness*, calls "delicate vibratories"). Wheatley's poetry is easily interpreted as the desire for cultivated taste, but when Giovanni and Wheatley meet in the "elsewhere" of African American literature, we gain a new way of understanding Wheatley as the origin of the struggle to cultivate taste for form-as-feeling in African American literature. Wheatley cultivates the taste for form-as-feeling in the midst of her performance of cultivated taste and mastery of the forms that cultivated her as a slave.

During the 1960s and early 1970s Black Arts Movement, Wheatley is resurrected as black scholars such as William H. Robinson begin to periodize African American literature through a focus on Wheatley's poetry as the beginning of a literary tradition.

The Vibrations of African American Literature

The cover of Robinson's study of Wheatley, *Phillis Wheatley in the Black American Beginnings*, has an image of a rope that has been cut but continues to have the tightness of knots and the motion of curves and turns. This image conveys the power of Wheatley's vibrations as her poetry continues to be the presence of absence (the cut space in this book cover image) that set the lyrical impulse of African American literature in motion.

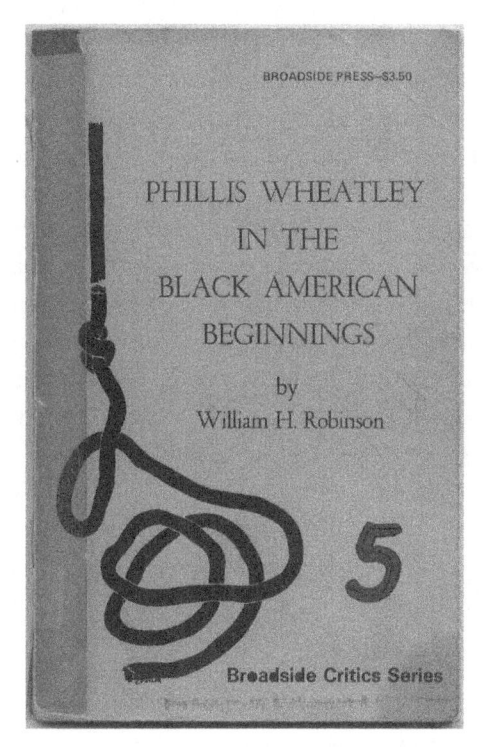

Figure 6. Broadside Press, 1975.

The Vibrations of *Cane*

Jean Toomer's *Cane* (1923), an African American literary classic, is claimed by a tradition even though Toomer insisted, after the publication of *Cane*, that he did not belong in a black literary tradition. *Cane* resides in African American literature but Toomer, after the publication of *Cane*, declared his exit from African American literature. The book remains a classic of African American literature but the author's post-*Cane* refusal to be framed as a "Negro" author has allowed the literal death of the author (the literal separation of the book and the author).

The move in and out of the lyrical, in *Cane*, signals a simultaneous sliding into and out of the black representational space that African American literature finally represented for Toomer. The simultaneous tone of the native informant and the anti-ethnographic poet emerges when language such as "Homes in Georgia are most often built on the two-room plan" appears alongside the lyrical language such as "Her skin is like dusk" in the opening portraits of *Cane*.[18] The native informant impulse epitomizes the anti-lyrical (the descriptive force that threatens to crush the black southern folk-spirit that pulls Toomer into the lyrical). Toomer famously describes the impetus for writing *Cane* in the following manner: "the folk-spirit was walking in to die on the modern desert. That spirit was so beautiful. Its death was so tragic. Just this seemed to sum life for me. And this was the feeling I put into 'Cane.' 'Cane' was a swan-song. It was a song of an end."[19] Toomer's emphasis on "this was the feeling I put into 'Cane'" matters. The text pivots on the unformed emotion that Toomer is struggling to express in words. The chant, in the opening portrait, "O cant you see it" transmutes, on the lower frequencies, into a call for the feeling of vibrations–"O cant you feel it."

Toomer, in the first section of *Cane*, make feeling vibrations a way of knowing the black southern folk-spirit. The feeling of vibrations creates the profound lyricism in the opening gallery of portraits of women. After *Cane*, Toomer could not be the legible writer he was before. He does not only become illegible in the color-line logic of identity, he also became illegible because the post-*Cane* writing was never able to make the mix of lyric and narrative work in the way that *Cane* made it work. In a 1929 journal entry, Toomer explains that his manuscript "Transatlantic" was not "carried" by "lyric feeling" in the way that *Cane* was. He writes, "Here is another mistake of *Transatlantic*: I believed I could carry it on a lyric feeling. I could not. I did not touch and tap the feelings, whatever they may have been, that would have carried it compellingly."[20] Vibrations of a lyrical, anti-narrative impulse within the structure of black narrative is what we feel in the deepest registers of the force field of African American literature. The tension between the lyrical and the narrative, in *Cane*, is also the tension between black abstraction and black representational space. *Cane* is Toomer's struggle to find access to black abstraction within black representational space.

Martin Puryear's *Cane* (2000), a twenty-first century visual art interpretation of *Cane*, brings to the surface the abstraction and representation tension that overdetermines the experimental impulse in *Cane*.[21] Puryear's visual art interpretation of *Cane* adds a new register to ways of understanding this classic of African American literature. His woodcuts carve out the tension between representation and abstraction and help us feel how Toomer fell in love, during the writing of *Cane*, with an idea of a black southern "folk-spirit" that was as real and abstract as black life being felt most as it dies. Toomer's words "the folk-spirit was walking in to die on the modern desert" (through the lens of Puryear's *Cane*-inspired art) becomes the "black abstraction that was walking in to die in representational space."[22]

Puryear's woodcuts give visual form to *Cane*'s tension between narrative and affect. In his woodcuts, we see the representational narratives that cannot explain the feeling that is too intense and unformed for Toomer to express it in a more direct manner. The lines in the woodcuts help us see and feel the practice of abstraction that makes the poetic lines in *Cane* burst out of narrative's confines. Puryear's woodcuts are an apt visual art attempt to *not* illustrate *Cane*. When *Cane* is trapped within an idea of African American literature that makes feeling a form of illustrating, we lose the ability to feel the practice of black abstraction in *Cane*. Puryear's woodcuts teach us how to read Toomer's post-*Cane* repudiation of the categorization "Negro literature" as Toomer's own

What is African American Literature?

practice of *cutting*. Toomer's literary practice of assemblage and cutting made him yearn for a way of assembling and cutting that could make one feel like a descendant of a tradition and, also, a creator of art that could never be contained by a rigid, respectable, color-line determined frame like the *tradition* of *Negro literature*.

Puryear's woodcut named "Fern" (after Toomer's "Fern") is a play with the capacity for curved lines to find loops. The woodcut makes the curved lines of connections and loops look like an abstract rendering of a huddle of bodies. In the right-hand corner of the woodcut, an arch with a vertical line in the middle looks like it is approaching the larger assemblage of curved lines and loops. The arch with the vertical line center has circles on its endpoints. One circle could touch one of the loops in the larger assemblage, if the arch moved just a bit closer to the larger formation.

The opening line in Toomer's "Fern" is a curved line: "Face flowed into her eyes" (14). The literal flow of the line circles from the abstraction "face" to her eyes. The first words in the second sentence--"Flowed in soft cream foam and plaintive ripples"— shape flow into a process of congealing and a process of movement. The simultaneity of the congealing and the movement is the tension that Puryear's woodcut captures. Toomer's "Fern" is a portrait of a young black woman whose beauty makes Toomer

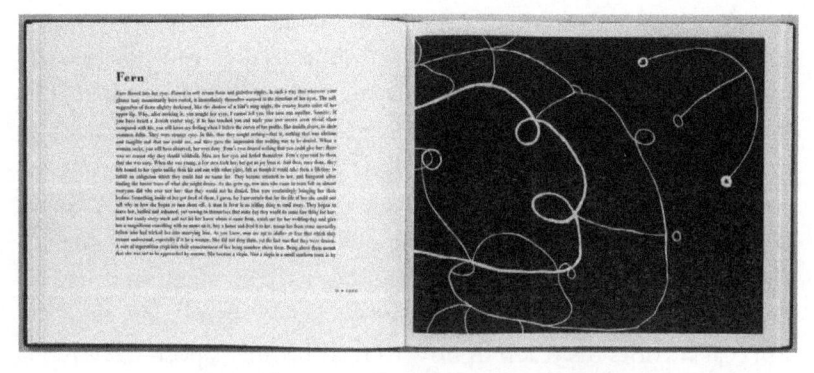

Figure 7.   Martin Puryear, Cane (2000)

88

feel the southern black "folk-spirit." The portrait is Toomer's heart-breaking attempt to show others this beauty that has almost shattered him. Toomer knows that words will fail him so he keeps adding more words to this portrait even as he knows that the eyes are the only part of this portrait that is congealing and approaching what he really yearns to say about Fernie May Rosen (whose full name we learn in the last sentence of this opaque portrait). Puryear's "Fern" woodcut helps us see Toomer's cut from foam and ripples to the narrator's ethnographic realism such as: "That the sexes were made to mate is the practice of the South. Particularly, black folks were made to mate. And it is black folks whom I have been talking about thus far" (15). This realism was the trap that made Toomer have to begin to leave the space of "Negro" literature as he entered into it. Toomer states these "facts" about the black South after he begins "Fern" with language that refuses all of this realism. He moves back and forth between the realism and the lyric abstraction. In Puryear's woodcuts, we see the move back and forth between the abstraction of marks and the impulse to create signs out of marks. Puryear opens up the tension in *Cane* between Toomer's drawn marks (the arcs), at the beginning of each section of the text, and the language in the text itself. The art historian James Elkins writes, "Marks exfoliate into fields and ultimately into surfaces, and they also gather surfaces into fields and finally into marks, so that visual artifacts are nothing but marks."[23] The arcs, included before each of *Cane*'s three sections, form an incomplete circle and signal a desire to let his words in *Cane* remain marks that will not congeal into a field of African American literature. Toomer's opening and closing words in the portrait "Carma" – "Wind is in the cane./ Come along." – are a call for an open field of air where we can feel mark-making becoming gestures that cannot be absorbed into a surface (10–11). Puryear's woodcuts are a visual interpretation of Toomer's "gathering" of marks, of partial images, that are a cut between black abstraction and the black figure ("Her skin is like dusk on the eastern horizon,/ O cant you see it, O cant you see it"(1)).

The cut between this realism and lyricism is not just a way of reading the deepest registers of *Cane*; it is also a way of understanding the feeling (the "beauty") that Alice Walker, in *In Search of Our Mothers' Gardens*, wants to hold onto even as she lets Toomer go: "*Cane* then is a parting gift, and no less precious because of that. I think Jean Toomer would want us to keep its beauty, but let him go" (65). Walker's desire to keep *Cane* but let Toomer go reminds us that the books that are "kept" in the *is-ness* of African American literature are not always viewed, by the authors, as belonging to that category. Toomer's frustration with the category "Negro literature" did not protect *Cane* from being fully absorbed into an African American literary canon.

The story of Toomer's complicated relationship to the production of African American literature brings us to the core question – what makes *Cane* seem so central in the tradition of African American literature? Why does *Cane* feel, for many readers, so indelibly "black"? The black abstraction in *Cane* emerges as the lyrical impulse pushes against the urge for more narratives that *capture* blackness. Toomer makes a black sublime emerge throughout the text. This sense of black awe is what makes *Cane* feel both so keepable (Alice Walker's language) and so ready to escape our grasp. This simultaneous holding and letting go is depicted in *Cane* itself as Toomer tries to capture the folk spirit as it is "walking in to die on the modern desert."[24] Keeping blackness and letting it go is, for Toomer, a profound contradiction that he does not resolve in *Cane* and this keeping and letting go is a dimension of the difference between the ephemeral idea of African American literature and the solid structure of African American literature. The fleeting idea of African American literature is dramatized in *Cane* and in Toomer's post-*Cane* repudiation of any investment in the category. Toomer's repudiation of the category opens up the deeper dimensions of the difference between the impulse to categorize and the impulse to honor a feeling that is pulling you in (a feeling-force that made Toomer write a book that pulled him all the way into blackness and, also, a book that pushed him all the way out of any need to identify as "negro" or "white").

The Vibrations of African American Literature

African American literature is a feeling force field. Just as Toomer, in the opening portraits in *Cane*, conveys the image of a magnetic force that is pulling in the narrator–spectator, the idea of Negro literature was a force field that pulled Toomer in and then made Toomer, after the publication of *Cane* and the framing of the book and author as "Negro," feel like he had to break out of this magnetic pull in order to remain free. Just as African American literature and the theme of blackness were a force field for Toomer, many other writers are pulled into this feeling force. The electric current keeps some writers spellbound by the idea of participating in the collective mood of African American literature, but some writers, like Toomer, are outside the force field and more able to honor the vibrations that do not settle into a force field of African American literature. Toomer's post-*Cane* writing delivers the vibrations. We learn more about the is-ness of African American literature when we let the vibrations of *Cane* in Toomer's post-*Cane* (post-African American literature) writing teach us how to honor feeling vibrations as a way of understanding the difference between an elusive *idea* of African American literature and an entirely legible *structure* of African American literature.

Once Toomer defied the re-production of *Cane* as a black text, a structure of African American literature continued to hold on to *Cane*, but does Toomer's repudiation of *Cane* as a black book change the structure that continues to contain *Cane*? If *Cane* is the *is-ness* of African American literature, not the structure of African American literature, how does the is-ness subvert the structure that contains it? The is-ness is what we feel in the prose poem "Rhobert" (in the second section of *Cane*) as Toomer differentiates between the house that Rhobert "wears" and the "stuffing that is alive" (40). As Rhobert wears the house like a helmet, he is pulled "way down" (40). The stuffing is what the structure tries to crush; the stuffing, for Toomer, is as light and ephemeral as the "folk-spirit walking in to die on the modern desert" (xxii). The house is described as "dead" (40). When Toomer defies the colorline logic of "Negro literature," the racializing of authorship seems deadening to him.

When Toomer makes the stuffing within the dead structure seem too ephemeral to be "stuff," he imagines an is-ness that is described in his post-*Cane* poem "The Lost Dancer" as the "vibrations of the dance [that] survive/ [t]he sand."[25] This image shapes a tradition of aesthetics into a tradition of vibrations that make what lingers as the shifting ground (the loose ground) of the tradition matter more than some type of holding on to the dancers who created the vibrations. Toomer writes: "Vibrations of the dance survive/ The sand; the sand, elect, survives/ The dancer" (39).

Toomer's use of dance to find access to the "is-ness" of vibrations gains new dimensions when his journal notes, in the archive at Beinecke Library, are read alongside the poem "The Lost Dancer." In a journal entry written in 1929, Toomer muses:

> Time and again I have noted a certain property in women who are dancers. […] It has to do with the way they handle their body; the way they view themselves. It is a false thing, a phony something which makes for posing and attitudinizing. I dislike it. I would like to take my fist and pound it out of them. It has nothing to do with a real sensing of the body, or with real movement, rhythm, sensuousness. […] These two often make these false movements, these posings and attitudinizings. A good deal of their behavior comes not from the sensuous spring of their body but from unfortunate ideas and pictures in their mind. […] A number of these dancers seem to have been arrested in the phase. With them it gives signs of being a permanent thing.[26]

Just as Toomer was frustrated with the intentional posing of dancers who cancelled out the "real sensing of the body," he was frustrated with being made a part of a structure of African American literature that converted the vibratory dance of his book into the arrested development of the still pose. Through the lens of the post-*Cane* poem "The Lost Dancer," the vibratory power of *Cane* is its refusal to bind sand on the feet. Toomer uses this image, in "The Lost Dancer," of moving sand that does not stick to the moving feet when he writes, "He can find no source/ Of magic adequate to bind/ The sand upon his feet" (39). When we heed Alice Walker's advice to keep *Cane* but let Toomer go, we are not keeping the sand; we are keeping the vibrations of his dance.

Toomer's vibrations of dance (in *Cane*) feel like the mystery of the lyrical struggling to not be swallowed by the narrative impulse to represent blackness in a clear and definitive manner. The attention to dance in the vignette "Theater" is one of the key moments when Toomer provides a meta-narrative that teaches us how to allow *Cane* to remain a part of a vibratory dance that we can call African American literature (and not a part of a *structure* that we need to call African American literature). In "Theater," Toomer foregrounds his frustration with the posing that makes some dance seem like "tricks" as opposed to the power of vibrations. Toomer writes, "Dorris dances. She forgets her tricks. [...] The walls press in, singing. Flesh of a throbbing body, they press close to John and Dorris. They close them in. John's heart beats tensely against her dancing body" (52-53). The vibratory power of the dance makes the walls almost implode as the intensity of the shared atmosphere loosens the solidity of the walls. The thoughts of John shift into a dreamscape as he watches Dorris dance. His experience of her dance breaks out of spectatorship and becomes the feeling of a shared atmosphere of vibrations. When Dorris' dance stops and John is no longer within the shared atmosphere of vibrations, Dorris "seeks for her dance" in John's face but "finds it a dead thing in the shadow which is his dream" (53). The deadness is the structure that crushes vibrations. Like Rhobert's helmet, the "dead thing" is what cancels out the "stuffing that is alive" (40).

The is-ness of African American literature is what Toomer found, as he wrote *Cane*, when he, like John in "Theater," felt pulled into a shared atmosphere of vibrations. The deadness of the category of African American literature was what Toomer detested when, after the publication of *Cane* and its steady framing as a "Negro" book, he felt his "whirls" (like Dorris' "whirls") being frozen and forced into a category that, for Toomer, created the falseness of dance that is more about posing than real movement ("a false thing, a phony something which makes for posing and attitudinizing").[27] Toomer, like this character John, was on the outskirts looking in at a dance that pulled him in and made him feel the vibrations of a black movement. When the dance ends and John would have to move from the vibrations of dance which he shared with Dorris to sharing Rhobert's helmet with Dorris, John can no longer participate in the movement that Dorris represents. Like John, Toomer was drawn into a collective movement but could not stay there once the dance stopped and a post-dance social structure demanded a way of talking that would be a shared discourse.

The feeling of blackness pulled Toomer in when it was a feeling of rupture and improvised movement, but once a publishing industry demanded that he add a "Negro signature" to his identity as an author, Toomer could not bear to sign his name and fix himself in a structure of African American literature. In a journal entry in the Beinecke archive, Toomer curses the entire color-line machine that makes his post-*Cane* writing be rejected by editors who cannot imagine that the new writing will hail a significant readership. He writes:

> My manuscript was returned with no results.
>   One of the men had read a French review of Cane. It appeared in Les Nouvelles Littéraires, just at this time, six years after the publication of the book. It called me a black poet, grouping me with Walrond and McKay.
>   [...] The review had to appear just at this time, of all the times during the past six years. It had to be read by the man who was considering my proposals and reading my manuscript!
>   This strange coincidence, the fact of Cane once again coming upon me and forcing me to realize the difficulty caused by my association with Negro, the failure of my project in which I had had sound reason to hope, shocked me from my comparative state of not feeling reality and made me again conscious of life as it is, of the real difficulties in managing this organism named Toomer.
>   But I did not sink under it. [...] But my spine not only remained straight but grew firmer. My emotional body took form. My feelings were sharp and strong. I moved into my own real world. I began really associating, thinking, perceiving, feeling, understanding, functioning.

[...] I cursed the man at the French Line, *Cane*, Waldo Frank, myself. [...] Most important, I realized as never before that the race business, to me, was an agent, a reliable main agent, of shocking [sic] and energizing me to consciousness of my main condition on earth, my purpose and aim in life. It brought me from the social into the objective world."[28]

This full passage teaches us how to feel the connections between the images of the oppressive house that Rhobert wears like a helmet and Toomer's relation to the color-line, "race business" of African American literature. This journal entry also lets us feel Toomer's escape from the "helmet." When he insists, "But I did not sink under it. [...] But my spine not only remained straight but grew firmer [...] My emotional body took form," we witness the move from an oppressive literary structure of containment to the formation of an "emotional body" (for Toomer, a way of describing the feelings that the "race business" could not crush). The words "my emotional body took form" are also a lucid way of thinking about the textual production of black affect, in *Cane*, that Toomer did not want contained by the race business of a literary establishment. African American literature, as an "emotional body" (a feeling force field) is what Toomer entered when he wrote *Cane*. Toomer never intended to enter into a structure and "race business" establishment called "African American literature."

For Toomer, making art within a "race business" was fundamentally antithetical to his understanding of the "stirring" of beauty that he depicted in the post-*Cane* poem "Angelic Eve" as "You stir [...],/ the silk as wings upon her feet,/ Emerging from undifferentiated air" (*The Collected Poems*, 41). When Toomer's intense but brief experience in Sparta, Georgia (as a Northern black person with a racially ambiguous body) produced the is-ness of *Cane*, Toomer found access to a black aesthetic experience of "undifferentiated air" (41). The black folk-spirit in Sparta, Georgia opened up a new dimension of feeling in Toomer. After *Cane* was absorbed by a race business of African American literature, Toomer felt that air was being stratified (a feeling force field was being crushed by a race machine).

When Puryear reshapes *Cane* into the wooden book of abstract woodcuts, *Cane* is literally reclaimed as too abstractly beautiful to be swallowed in a "race business." Puryear's woodcut drawing of Toomer's portrait "Esther" makes the vibratory power of lines speak to Toomer's image of Esther deciding that she loves Barlo (upon whom the young, "almost white" Esther projects so many fantasies of authentic blackness). Esther's decision to love Barlo dissipates at the end of the portrait when she realizes that "King Barlo" is a drunkard, but Puryear's woodcut lets the vibratory power of lines allow for a desire that can hold on to the "emotional body" of both Esther and Barlo.[29] Puryear's woodcut allows us to re-feel Toomer's image of Barlo's vibratory blackness ("magnetic" blackness) in "Esther" (23). In *Cane*, Toomer uses the power of vibratory blackness to push against the race business that makes Esther feel that she cannot simply fall in love with the is-ness of blackness (that she must choose to be in love with a structure of race that makes Barlo's blackness more authentic than her own).

To Choose and Lose Signature: Entering into the Not Yet Here

John Keene and Christopher Stackhouse's *Seismosis* (2006) invites readers to enter into a book of vibrations. The word "signature" is used throughout this word-and-image text as the seismic signature of vibrations becomes the core tension of the book. The title of the book is a playful mix of the words "semiosis" and "seismology." Keene's poetry and Stackhouse's drawings create an earthquake rupture of any narrow idea of the boundaries between African American visual art and African American literature.

As Keene and Stackhouse create the mix of semiosis and seismology, they allow the study of signs to merge with the study of earthquakes. The vibratory power of African American literature emerges, in this word-and-image text, as the lines (in the poetry and drawings) do not create recognizable structures but seismic waves that explore the ways in which the structure of black art needs marks and lines to always become signs. *Seismosis* shows that the idea of black art is the earthquake that crushes the investment in a structural approach to African American literature. The idea of black art is the idea that a tradition of mark-making does not need to be consolidated into a normative way of understanding tradition.

Throughout *Seismosis*, Keene repeats the words "mark event" and "signature" and ultimately allows the book's final rupture to be the idea that black art may be a "mark event" in which one can "choose and lose signature."[30] The structure of African American literature demands a clear and legible signature. The idea of African American literature demands the ability to imagine what the *feeling force field* was before it was consolidated into the structure of literary tradition. Keene and Stackhouse perform the difference between the signature that has always already been written and the suspended process of signing that makes marks look like they have not congealed yet into a recognizable sign. *Seismois* teaches us how to feel the "not yet here," emergent idea of African American literature. What will African American literature become? How does the not yet here shape what African American literature *is*?

In *Seismosis*, the imprint of the not yet here on the is-ness can be felt in the seismic waves of Stackhouse's line drawings as they become ways of sketching without a preconceived organized idea. The is-ness of the drawings is not what the lines and curves have produced but what the lines and curves might produce if the book successfully hails the emergence of a type of readership that may not exist yet. Keene's poetry, like the line drawings in *Seismosis*, makes the *not yet here* feel like it is already present. The earthquake that *Seismosis* performs is this making present of what is still emerging. This word-and-image book makes twenty-first century African American literature seem like the practice of letting the emergent remain emergent. Through the lens of *Seismosis*, the idea of African American literature is the idea of breaking out of the "tradition of African American literature" in order to feel the experimental impulse that has always been the vibrating force of the tradition. Keene only includes the word "black" in three poems in this text that refuses to announce any attention to black identity. In "Self," one of the three poems that includes the word "black," the question is posed – "Self, black self, is there another label?" (19). This poem ends with the following asterisked words:

> *To precisely describe all configurations, positionalities, and momenta, he draws the black images to shore up these parameters.
>   *In the end, refuse signature. (19)

When we think of this book as a part of the not-yet-here of African American literature, it might be that we are feeling the book "shore up" that which is still emerging. To shore up the not-yet-here is to feel the vibrations of what is coming. *Seismosis* lets us dream of a day when African American literature may lose any tie to the "*I need to prove my humanity/ I need to write myself into existence*" transaction at the core of the historical structure of African American literature. In *Seismosis*, the emphasis on refusing (and losing) signature leads us to the end of this "transaction" and the letting go of any need to treat vibrations as the tidy signs and marks of a cohesive African American literary history. The title of the book, the neologism "seismosis," stages the battle between the study of signs (semiosis) and the study of seismic waves (seismology). Keene and Stackhouse situate the is-ness of the not-yet-here as the wave-making that does not need to be read as sign-making. As a feeling force field, what is African American literature? It is an emotional history of waves of feeling blackness. These emotional waves are profoundly misunderstood when, instead of being felt as a vibratory power, they are treated as walls in a structure that makes writers feel stuck as Toomer did post-*Cane*.

"Selves echo in my fracture zone" is one of the most resonant lines in *Seismosis* (60). African American literature is a "fracture zone." Fracture zones "are valleys that cut across midocean ridges, thus providing a passage for flow of cold bottom water from one ocean basin to another."[31] The is-ness of African American literature is the passage of lyrical echoes, in "cold bottom water," from one text to another. It is the practice of shiver explored in the next chapter.

Endnotes

1. Quoted in: Addison Gayle, ed. *The Black Aesthetic* (New York: Doubleday, 1971), 15.
2. Fred Moten, "The Case of Blackness," *Criticism*, Volume 50, Number 2, Spring 2008, 182.
3. Stephen Henderson, *Understanding the New Black Poetry: Black Speech and Black Music as Poetic References* (New York: William Morrow & Company, Inc., 1973), 66.
4. In *Theory of the Lyric*, Jonathan Culler writes, "Poetics and hermeneutics may be difficult to separate in practice, but in theory they are quite distinct: they come at literature from opposite directions" (5).
5. Phillis Wheatley, *Poems on Various Subjects, Religious and Moral* (Middletown, DE: Pantianos Classics, 2017 [1773]), 18.
6. Alexis Pauline Gumbs, *M Archive: After the End of the World* (Durham and London: Duke University Press, 2018), 122.
7. Vertamae Grosvenor, *Vibration Cooking: or the Travel Notes of a Geechee Girl* (Garden City, NY: Doubleday, Inc., 1970), n.p.
8. Alice Walker, *In Search of Our Mothers' Gardens* (New York: Harcourt, Inc., 2003 [1983]), 237.
9. https://id.erudit.org/iderudit/038761a
Trower writes, "Focusing initially on Coleridge's "The Aeolian Harp" (first composed in 1795), I track how the harp as a metaphor for the sensitive and imaginative, creative poet, corresponds with Hartley's materialist account of both perception and creativity, of receptive and responsive motions, or 'incoming' and 'outgoing' vibrations."
10. Rowan Ricardo Phillips, *When Blackness Rhymes with Blackness* (Champaign and London: Dalkey Archive Press, 2010), 16.
11. Nikki Giovanni, *Those Who Ride the Night Winds* (New York: Quill, 1983), 27.
12. Margaret Walker and Nikki Giovanni, *A Poetic Equation: Conversations Between Nikki Giovanni and Margaret Walker* (Washington, D.C.: Howard University Press, 1974), 76–77.198
13. Nikki Giovanni, *Love Poems* (New York: William Morrow, Inc., 1997), 19.
14. Fred Moten, "Jurisgenerative Grammar (for Alto)" in *The Oxford Handbook of Critical Improvisation*, ed. George E. Lewis and Benjamin Piekut (New York: Oxford University Press, 2016), 133.

What is African American Literature?

15 In their unpublished work on dance, gesture, and affect, Dixon Li uses this phrase "stranded affect."
16 Larry Neal, *Hoodoo Hollerin' Bebop Ghosts* (Washington, D.C.: Howard University Press, 1974), 54.
17 Kevin Young, *Blues Poems* (New York: Random House, 2003), 11.
18 Jean Toomer, *Cane* (New York: Liveright, 1975 [1923]), 1.
19 Darwin T. Turner, ed. *The Wayward and the Seeking: A Collection of Writings by Jean Toomer* (Washington., D.C.: Howard University Press, 1982), 123.
20 Jean Toomer Papers. James Weldon Johnson Collection. Beinecke Rare Book and Manuscript Library. https://archives.yale.edu/repositories/11/resources/950, Series II, 1929 file.
21 Arion Press collaborated with Martin Puryear, in 2000, to create a new edition of *Cane* with woodcut prints. Puryear created visual interpretations of seven portraits in *Cane*. Arion Press created 400 copies of this new edition of *Cane*. Puryear's seven woodblock portraits are created out of African wenge, Swiss pear, Italian walnut, and New England maple.
22 Darwin T. Turner, ed. *The Wayward and the Seeking: A Collection of Writings by Jean Toomer* (Washington.,D.C.: Howard University Press, 1982), 123.
23 James Elkins, "Marks, Traces, 'Traits,' Contours, 'Orli,' and 'Splendores': Nonsemiotic Elements in Pictures," *Critical Inquiry*, Vol. 21, No. 4 (Summer, 1995), 845.
24 Darwin T. Turner, ed. *The Wayward and the Seeking* (Washington., D.C.: Howard University Press, 1982), 123.
25 Robert B. Jones and Margery Toomer Latimer, ed. *The Collected Poems of Jean Toomer* (Chapel Hill & London: The University of North Carolina Press, 1988), 39.
26 Jean Toomer Papers. James Weldon Johnson Collection. Beinecke Rare Book and Manuscript Library. https://archives.yale.edu/repositories/11/resources/950, Series II, 1929 file.
27 Jean Toomer Papers. James Weldon Johnson Collection. Beinecke Rare Book and Manuscript Library. https://archives.yale.edu/repositories/11/resources/950, Series II, 1929 file.
28 Jean Toomer Papers. James Weldon Johnson Collection. Beinecke Rare Book and Manuscript Library. https://archives.yale.edu/repositories/11/resources/950, 20 Sept 1929 file.

29 Jean Toomer Papers. James Weldon Johnson Collection. Beinecke Rare Book and Manuscript Library. https://archives.yale.edu/repositories/11/resources/950, 20 Sept 1929 file.
30 John Keene and Christopher Stackhouse, *Seismosis*. (Chicago: 1913 Press, 2006),1, 103.
31 https://www.sciencedirect.com/topics/earth-and-planetary-sciences/fracture-zone

4

Shiver: The Diasporic Shock of Elsewhere

> We all know that we have feelings when we encounter works of art. We laugh, we cry. We feel pity and fear. We like and we dislike. We shudder and shiver and tingle.
> —Jonathan Flatley, "Reading for Mood"

> To bend with the tight intentness
> over the neat detail, come to
> a terrified standstill of the heart, then shiver […]
> —Gwendolyn Brooks, *In the Mecca*

When Zora Neale Hurston wrote *Their Eyes Were Watching God* in Haiti, she was attempting to recover from the recent end of a relationship that she described as the "real love affair of my life."[1] Hurston was hurting, and writing the love story in Haiti (*Their Eyes Were Watching God*) made her feel that she was being directed by a "force somewhere in Space."[2] Her description of this unlocatable force should make us consider *Their Eyes Were Watching God* (a classic in the African American literary tradition) as a novel that finds its beauty in what Edouard Glissant calls the "shock of elsewhere."[3] Glissant muses, "The power to experience the shock of elsewhere is what distinguishes the poet" (29–30). This language used to describe the poetic impulse (in *Poetics of Relation*) opens up

What is African American Literature?, First Edition. Margo N. Crawford.
© 2021 John Wiley & Sons, Inc. Published 2021 by John Wiley & Sons, Inc.

the role of diaspora in African American literature. Glissant has famously theorized diaspora as open "Relation" and a web of roots that reframes the logic of the question – "relation between what and what?" (27). Glissant describes black diasporic aesthetic flows as "fleeting, delicate shivers," as involuntary, subtle impulses (159). Like a shiver, a diasporic impulse continues to move through the national boundaries of African American literature. The shiver of the poetic impulse, for Glissant, is the "shock of elsewhere" (30).

In African American literature, there is a steady tension between black diasporic shivers and black diasporic narratives that freeze these shivers. Edwidge Danticat remembers announcing, when she was young, to her classmates: "Zora has lived in my country," [...] and now I am living in hers."[4] Amiri Baraka has famously stated, "In America, black *is* a country."[5] When we connect his words and Danticat's, we feel both the transmutation of the idea of nation into the idea of culture and the potential crushing of the shared elsewhere of African American and Caribbean literature through the imagined "country" of blackness. Glissant worries about this potential freezing of the shiver of elsewhere. He writes, "Our obligation to 'grasp' violence, often fight it, estranges us from such live intensity, as it also freezes the shiver and disrupts prescience. But this force never runs dry because it is its own turbulence" (159). The impulse to not freeze the diasporic shivers of blackness is the most radical zone of the global black consciousness in African American literature. The "fleeting, delicate shivers" remain unfrozen as diaspora continues to be the "shock of elsewhere" that we sometimes stumble upon in African American literature.

In *Americanah* (2013), Chimamanda Adichie's main character, Ifemelu, writes a blog about the all-absorbing nature of the word "Black" in the American context. Ifemelu writes, in this blog, "To My Fellow Non-American Blacks: In America, You Are Black, Baby."[6] These words have gained a greater resonance as this novel, in America, continues to shape twenty-first century understandings of literature that is "African" and "American." In "Bye-Bye Barbar" (2005), Taiye Selasi describes Adichie as a "twenty-first century African."[7] As Selasi

Shiver: *The Diasporic Shock of Elsewhere*

describes the "afropolitan" ethos of writers such as Adichie, she argues that this new generation of "Afropolitans – not citizens, but Africans, of the world" become black based on "where we locate ourselves in the history that produced 'blackness' and the political processes that continue to shape it" (530). In *Americanah*, Adichie locates and dislocates "African" and "African American." This classic twenty-first century Afropolitan novel is also a signature text in the landscape of twenty-first century African American literature.

There is a profound tension in the novel between the blog world of decoding blackness and the more subtle gestures to affect that make us shiver and feel the shock of elsewhere. At the beginning of the novel, Ifemelu is preparing to return to Lagos. She feels disoriented by the illogic of race in America. She reads *Cane* as she is preparing to return to Lagos. Toomer's two months in Sparta, Georgia (the experience that led to *Cane*) makes him feel that the "folk-spirit was walking in to die on the modern desert."[8] Ifemelu feels that "Americanah" is the "modern desert." We wonder if Toomer's depiction of the evanescent, painful beauty of the black southern folk-spirit speaks to Ifemelu. Amiri Baraka describes the South, in *Blues People*, as "the scene of the crime" (the scene of slavery).[9] The unknowable "scene" of the Global South may be on Ifemelu's mind as she reads Toomer's images of the black South in the northern black imagination. Adichie foregrounds Ifemelu's reading of *Cane* in a hair braiding salon as she prepares to return to Lagos. The character's reading of *Cane* is a "fleeting, delicate shiver" that is repeated but never developed into any explanation of the character's feelings about the book (Glissant 159). The impact of the citation lingers because Ifemelu's reading of the book is a state of suspension. After many chapters of flashback, we return to the beauty salon scene and Ifemelu continues to read *Cane*.

The shiver of this fleeting gesture to *Cane* in *Americanah* opens up the shiver of *Cane* itself that remains unfrozen in spite of all of the narratives trying to freeze it. Why does Adichie make *Cane* the shiver of suspension, the mysterious scene of Ifemelu's reading suspension? In *Americanah*, Ifemelu's blogs are representational space.

The blogs are a constant play with a public discourse of blackness, black hair, the Obamas, the naturalized differences between non-American blacks and American blacks, etc.

In the blogs, Ifemelu makes blackness into an object of study. In contrast, there are other, fleeting moments in the novel when blackness is only claimed through the shiver of affect, not through the public discourse that the blogs represent. In "Bye-Bye Barbar," Selasi proposes that the difference between the older generations' and afropolitans' relation to home is the fact, for the younger afropolitans, home and identity are a "matter of affect" (530). Selasi writes, "While our parents can claim one country as home, we must define our relationship to the places we live: how British or American we are (or act) is in part a matter of affect" (530). In the blogs, Ifemelu continues to define and explain the difference between "American blacks" and "non-American blacks." In the parts of the novel that break out of this explanatory blog discourse, Adichie relies on the "matter of affect" (530). When she makes affect matter than the blogs, the novel breaks the affective boundaries between African and African American literature. We feel the expansion of the "African American literature" frame as it becomes large enough to intersect with the frame "African literature." The fleeting references to *Cane* are the quintessential anti-blog moments in the novel. Adichie makes Ifemelu's connection to *Cane* an unexplainable "matter of affect" (Selasi 530). Like Toomer's resonant words "O cant [sic] you see it," Adichie pulls readers into the horizon of African *and* American literature.

In the short story "Shivering" (2009), Adichie begins with the shivering that happens as a young woman, Ukamaka, is praying with a stranger who feels the prayer in a way that she cannot. As the stranger holds her hands, Ukamaka "felt awkward with her hands clasped together, his fingers warm and firm."[10] When she starts shivering, the prayer makes Ukamaka feel Glissant's "shock of elsewhere" in her own body. Adichie writes, "Then she felt herself start to shiver, an involuntary quivering of her whole body" (144). In *Americanah*, Adichie performs the shiver of the "whole body" of African and African American literature.

Shiver: *The Diasporic Shock of Elsewhere*

Ama Ata Aidoo performs the diasporic shock of elsewhere in *Our Sister Killjoy* (1977), her novel-like, prose poem that stands out in African literature as one of the most experimental and innovative texts. This experimental prose poem pivots on affect such as shiver and blush. Aidoo writes, "When Sissie lifted her head and their eyes met, red blood rushed into Marija's face. So deeply red. Sissie felt embarrassed for no reason that she knew. The atmosphere changed."[11] Aidoo shapes *Our Sister Killjoy* around the shared atmosphere of affect. She teaches us how to feel the black diaspora as a shared atmosphere of shivers (expressed as Our Sister Killjoy's frustration with the frozen, colonized minds) and the shared atmosphere of black blush (expressed at the very end of the book when "My Precious Something" says, "I know everyone calls you Sissie, but what is your name?") The possibility of black blush is situated as the possibility of black love.

Aidoo's practice of black diasporic shiver emerges when she begins the final section entitled "A Love Letter," with the following exchange:

> Said an anxious Afro-American student to a visiting professor, 'Sir, please, tell me: is Egypt in Africa?'
> 'Certainly,' replied the professor.
> 'I mean Sir, I don't mean to kind of harass you or anything,' pressed the student, 'but did the Egyptians who built the pyramids, you know, the Pharaohs and all, were they African?'
> 'My dear young man,' said the visiting professor, 'to give you the decent answer your anxiety demands, I would have to tell you a detailed history of the African continent. And to do that, I shall have to speak every day, twenty-four hours a day, for at least three thousand years. And I don't mean to be rude to you or anything, but who has that kind of time?'
>
> (111)

Why is this student marked as "Afro-American"? We might rush to quick and easy assumptions about the tendency of African

What is African American Literature?

Americans to romanticize Africa and crave the idea of "black Africa" and prelapsarian Africa, or we may read this passage as a shiver, a state of suspension, in which Aidoo makes us feel a jolt of electricity in the words "but who has that kind of time?" The words "to give you the decent answer your anxiety demands" show that Aidoo is searching for words that do not pathologize the question delivered by the "Afro-American student." The professor cannot produce the "detailed history" that the "anxiety demands." The professor's alternative offering is a diasporic shock of dispossession (not *having* that kind of time) that can only be felt when we become exhausted with "that detailed history kind of time" and remain open to what black diasporic "anxiety demands" (111).

The words, "but who has that kind of time," illuminate the reason why Aidoo begins *Our Sister Killjoy* with the tension of slow motion (as readers pause and zoom in on the few words on each page and the overwhelming white space without words) and a cinematic flow (a sense of words in motion like moving pictures that make readers turn the first pages in a quick manner since there are so few words on each page). This tension between slow motion reading and cinematic flow creates the feeling that time is out of joint in the literary space of black radicalism:

> Things are working out [first page]
> [...]
> toward their dazzling conclusions... [second page]
> [...]
> ...so it is neither here nor there,
> what ticky-tackies we have
> saddled and surrounded ourselves with,
> blocked our views,
> cluttered our brains [third page]
> [...]
> What is frustrating, though, in arguing with a nigger who is a 'moderate' is that since... [fourth page][12]

Shiver: *The Diasporic Shock of Elsewhere*

On the fourth opening page, Aidoo breaks out of the sparse words on pages that are predominantly white space. With the words "What is frustrating," she begins to move to the normative use of the full page for words; words fill more than half of the fourth opening page. When the question from the "Afro-American student" appears much later in the text, Aidoo makes the reader return to the tension between suspended time and quickly moving pages performed in the opening sequence of the text. The presence of the "Afro-American" within the "African" text is framed as a "fleeting, delicate shiver" (Glissant 159).

In the play *The Dilemma of a Ghost* (1964), Ama Ata Aidoo depicts the freezing of the emergent "fleeting, delicate shivers" of black diasporic feminism in a narrative of compulsory reproduction. This play depicts young newlyweds' life in Ghana after meeting at an American university. The couple is an African American woman and a Ghanaian man. Eulalie, the African American woman, wants to wait before having a child. The family of the Ghanaian husband, Ato, assumes that she is incapable of having a child. Ato knows that his family will not understand that a woman can choose when she will become a mother. In the final act, he tells his mother the truth – that he and his wife have chosen to not have a child. In this 1960s Black Power-era play, Aidoo disrupts the US Black Power Movement imagery of the black women's body as the reproductive motherland and hails a black feminism tied to reproductive choice. The end of the play, however, pivots on the after-effects of the husband slapping his wife after she "said that my people have no understanding, that they are uncivilized."[13] The depiction of the slap conveys the violent diasporic shivers that give Glissant's words "the shock of elsewhere" another meaning. The stage directions read:

> [Like the action of lightning, ATO smacks her on the cheek and goes out of the house going by the path on the left. EULALIE, stunned, holds her cheeks in her hands for several seconds. She tries to speak but the words do not come. She crumples, her body

shaking violently with silent tears, into the nearest chair. This goes on for a while and then the lights go out.] (48)

The play makes us wonder about the future of Eulalie's shaking. How might a black diasporic feminism allow the "dilemma of the ghost" to not be solved by the normative, patriarchal kinship rules of reproduction? Ato's sister connects Eulalie to the lyrics in a song that freezes any possibility of black feminist shiver: "She is strange/ She is unusual/ She would have done murder/ Had she been a man/ But to prevent/ Such an outrage/ They made her a woman!/ Look at a female!" (33). Aidoo's *The Dilemma of a Ghost*, like Adichie's *Americanah*, troubles the narratives that set African literature apart from African American literature. *The Dilemma of a Ghost* breaks the boundaries between African drama and African American drama.

In *Swing Time* (2016), Zadie Smith creates a literary space in-between the African, Black British, and African American. Smith's *Swing Time* (2016) cuts from England to the United States and West Africa as she uses dance as a means of thinking about the actual *practice* of diaspora as an embodied practice. Smith depicts the complex soulmate and soul-killing friendship, from childhood to adulthood, between two girls (and, later, women) who fall in love with life through their love of dance. Dance emerges as an alternative form of kinship. When the young narrator envies the ability of her friend, Tracey, to attend a school for dance (not the more academically rigorous one that her mother forces her to attend), she thinks, "In my mind, her struggles were over. She was a dancer: she'd found her tribe."[14] In a key passage, Smith shapes the issue of dance as alternative kinship around the power of the shock of elsewhere. She writes:

> The greatest dancer I ever saw was the kankurang. But in the moment I didn't know who or what it was: a wildly swaying orange shape, of a man's height but without a man's face, covered in many swishing, overlapping leaves. Like a tree in the blaze of a New York fall that uproots itself and now dances down the street. (163).

Shiver: *The Diasporic Shock of Elsewhere*

Smith's unnamed narrator is in an unnamed West Africa country at this point in the narrative. Smith gives us clues to where the narrator may be. We know that she is not too far from Senegal. Smith's refusal to name the location may be a means of stressing how *moved* elsewhere the narrator feels, as this dancer and the music make the narrator's body move. Affect is at the core of *Swing Time* as the entire diasporic flow of the novel becomes a question of what Smith describes as "felt history." Felt history is the zone that Smith's narrator describes as "a different kind of history from my mother's, the kind that is barely written down—that is felt" (101).

In *A Map to the Door of No Return: Notes to Belonging*, Dionne Brand writes: "Flung out and dispersed in the Diaspora, one has a sense of being touched by or glimpsed from this Door. As if walking down a street someone touches you on the shoulder but when you look around there is no one, yet the air is oddly warm with some live presence."[15] Brand fully approaches the idea of an "oddly warm" shiver as she describes "flung out" diasporic subjects gaining the sensation of being, somehow, connected by a diasporic consciousness. Brand offers (with this emphasis on the Middle Passage and touch) a Middle Passage phenomenology that, due to the ephemerality and lightness of touch, could never become the hegemonic Middle Passage epistemology that Michelle Wright critiques in *The Physics of Blackness: Beyond the Middle Passage Epistemology*.[16] How could diasporic touch ever be historicized? Brand is right to focus on the air (on the presence of absence). When the word "Black" is most tied to the power of the oddly warm shiver, we can feel Glissant's diasporic web of roots (the rhizome) as a web of touches. What kind of alternative black solidarity has been created through this alternative kinship of touch? What makes the "flung out" diasporic subject feel black (*or shiver black*)?

The black diaspora is, through lens of Nadia Ellis' *Territories of the Soul: Queered Belonging in the Black Diaspora* (2015), a "belonging forged out of intense affect and eccentric forms of intimacy."[17] The forms of belonging that shape the diasporic dimension of African

What is African American Literature?

American literature are the unpredictable creases created as literary imaginations tied to sites such as Africa, the Caribbean, Europe and the United States fold into each other. The practice of working with the folds and creases is seen when Lucille Clifton, in the poem "Study the Masters," imagines a black American woman poet's labor with the iron as a way of understanding "America." Clifton writes:

> like my aunt timmie.
> it was her iron,
> or one like hers,
> that smoothed the sheets
> the master poet slept on.
> home or hotel, what matters is
> he lay himself down on her handiwork
> and dreamed. she dreamed too, words:
> some cherokee, some masai and some
> huge and particular as hope.
> if you had heard her
> chanting as she ironed
> you would understand form and line
> and discipline and order and
> america.[18]

The gestures to diaspora, in African American literature, are gestures to the folds and creases that create both the radical practices of global black consciousness in African American literature and, also, the hegemonic practices of exporting "African Americanness" to other parts of the black diaspora. The unironed diasporic creases or folds, in African American literature, differ from the images of the enfoldment and absorption of other sites of diaspora in the zone of African American literature. The tension between writing with a diasporic edge and writing to "iron the wrinkles of the diaspora" shapes many practices of diaspora in African American literature. African American writers have consciously or unconsciously subsumed other parts of the black diaspora in an African American narrative, but African American writers have also created a diasporic literary openness.

Shiver: *The Diasporic Shock of Elsewhere*

Beyond the Impulse to Anthologize: the Shiver of What is Left Out

The tension between the impulse to subsume and the shiver of vulnerability and openness overdetermines the practice of diaspora in African American literature. The practice of subsumption is seen most clearly when images of blackness (in African American literature) make blackness mean African Americanness. The correspondence between Bessie Head and Langston Hughes, during 1960–1961, shows how African American literature and African literature have sometimes become each other's conditions of possibility. The diasporic shiver emerges as Head and Hughes create the "fleeting, delicate" space in the letters for the sharing of a blues that is African American and South African (Glissant 159). In one letter, Hughes writes, "Perhaps you have heard an American Negro blues that says, "The sun's gonna shine in my back door someday." And Head responds, "Yes I know that blues—'The Sun's gonna shine'— Dinah Washington and co. But how can you doubt that you will not live to see your back door lit up?"[19] Bessie Head writes to Hughes because she views him as someone who will understand the urgency of her writing and her urgent need to get it published. After she quotes lines from his poem "As I Grew Older," she writes: "The idea for this book was nurtured by such a feeling of despair, absolute frustration and a deep sense of isolation, of not belonging" (8). Head and Hughes meet in the space of "not belonging." In the space of suspension created by the letter-writing (where they meet in the shock of elsewhere), Hughes is not situated in the ground of African Americanness and Head is not situated in the ground of South Africanness. They meet elsewhere as their letters take us to the edge of African and African American literature.

In her first letter to Hughes, Head cites the following lines from Hughes' poem "As I Grew Older":

As I grew older—
No more the light of my dream before me,
The wall!

What is African American Literature?

My black hands!
I lay down in the shadow of the wall! (8)

Imagine Head reading Hughes's description of "lay[ing] down in the shadow of the wall" and feeling that she knows that shadow although she has been shaped by other walls. The shared shadow is the shared shock of elsewhere. In the letters that Head and Hughes send each other, we can feel how Glissant's "fleeting, delicate shiver" could easily be frozen by an American operation of race and an American operation of black literature. When Head explains the divide and conquer, in South Africa, between those categorized as "African" and "Colored," Hughes responds with an emphasis on the culture of the one drop rule in the United States. As Head and Hughes compare the racial logic that shape the two countries, Head cites Hughes' words "My black hands!" as if she wants their hands to touch in the shock of elsewhere.

In one of the letters, Hughes confesses to Head that he is poor as she is (when she asks him for assistance with beginning to shape her life around her writing and publishing). As they both reach out, in these letters, to touch what they are too far away from to know, they create a feeling of togetherness without the actual experience of intimacy. Hughes tells her that the photograph she sent to him is displayed on his mantle.

> Your striking picture is on my mantle piece in front of my desk right now. I hope you get to come to New York sometime to see us here in person.
> Your book sounds like a fine and helpful idea. But its interest and appeal would be, I think, from the way you describe it, largely for readers in your own country—where, as you indicate, such a book is needed. (9)

African American literature is a "fine and helpful idea," for Head, as she begins her journey toward becoming one of the most experimental and innovative African writers who greatly expand the space of the category "African literature."

Shiver: *The Diasporic Shock of Elsewhere*

In 1949, years before this letter-writing between Hughes and Head, *The Poetry of the Negro* is edited by Hughes and Arna Bontemps. This anthology delivers a very narrow vision of the category of African poetry. There are only three poems in the "Africa" section, all written by a Ghanaian poet. This anthology frames "Negro" poetry as African American, Caribbean, and the "tribute" work of white poets ("Tributary Poems by Non-Negroes").[20] In their introduction, Hughes and Bontemps explain that the racial formation of the United States differs from that in other sites of the black diaspora and that their anthology will not attempt to translate these differences and produce some type of shared racial identification. In spite of this processing of the differences in the introduction, the anthology does lapse into an American operation of race. The anthology expands the idea of African American literature, through the production of the "poetry of the Negro" as the capaciousness of African American literature (as African American literature being touched by many other sites of poetic production). The anthology does not allow this touching to be felt in a multidirectional manner. The move from African American poetry to the other poetry traditions makes African American literature the implied source that sets the other poetry traditions in motion (the source that has been touched by all the other non-African American poets). But things fall apart in the final, fleeting, delicate shiver of "Africa" (the final three poems written by Aquah Laluah). Laluah's poems are a *shock of elsewhere* in this anthology. Her poems stand without any other "family" members. Her last poem "The Souls of Black and White" presents blackness and whiteness as the "selfsame shade" (385). The anthology ends with a delicate shiver of universalism that makes the anthologizing (the gathering and collection) of "The Poetry of the Negro" fall apart, in the last pages, and become the poetry of the "selfsame shade" (385). This tension between the anthologizing and the falling apart continues to shape the enterprise of African American literature as the impulse to frame the literary tradition continues to produce the aesthetic shock of elsewhere.

What is African American Literature?

Hughes and Bontemps anthologize African American poetics (and the idea of African American literature) in a manner that makes "the poetry of negro" seem like an American operation of race and identity. In a similar manner, Hughes' editing of *An African Treasury* (1960) makes the idea of African literature seem like an African American collection of the idea of African literature. In the introduction, as Hughes explains the openness of his collection process, he writes:

> To correspondents and to fans of my own work in Africa—where over the years my poems have been published and my 'Simple' stories serialized—I wrote for the addresses of native writers. To Prime Minister Azikiwe's chain of newspapers in Nigeria I sent a letter asking for contributions to a proposed anthology. My request was reprinted in numerous papers in other parts of Africa. Within a few weeks I began to receive floods of material from all over English-speaking Africa.[21]

The openness of Hughes' collection process collides with the machine that his African Americanness becomes as he necessarily, as editor, becomes the arbiter of what can exist within this "African treasury." This "machine" of the American collection process gains a new spin when Hughes explains, in the introduction, that one of the African writers hoping to be included in this "treasury" states the following in his letter to Hughes: "But I hope soon to exploit the art of typewriting for the happy sake of the musical rhythms it produces when man beats the machine" (xi). This writer, who remains unnamed in this introduction, initially sends handwritten poems to Hughes. His reference to "beating the machine" is a reference to using a typewriter, but, on the meta-level, it is also a powerful way of thinking about the "machine" of Americanizing that would crush the is-ness of both African American literature and African literature.

How do we ever break out of the machine that naturalizes the space between "African" and "American" in the idea of "African American literature"? How do we move to the multi-directional collection and influence of African and African American literature?

Shiver: *The Diasporic Shock of Elsewhere*

The Diasporic Shivers of Keorapetse Kgositsile

The practice of the shock of elsewhere of Keorapetse Kgositsile was profoundly *African* and *American*.[22] A different way of thinking about the idea of "African (and) American literature" emerges when it is viewed from the perspective of people situated in a diasporic travel that often led to the liminal work across movements and across continents.

Before analyzing Kgositsile's poetics of the diasporic shock of elsewhere, an account of his travel is necessary. A year after the 1960 Sharpeville massacre, Kgositsile, a young ANC member, was advised to leave South Africa if he wanted to write without fear of imprisonment or surveillance. He first moved to Dar Es Salaam, Tanzania in order to be a part of the black consciousness-raising tied to *Spearhead* magazine, a pan-African newspaper-style magazine that was sold "in the streets" from 1961 to 1963. After Tanzania, he moved to the United States, studying briefly at Lincoln University in Pennsylvania and then, in 1962, moving to New York. From 1962–1975, he lived in exile in the United States. When the ANC recommended that Kgositsile become an exile, the apartheid regime was heightening its ideological violence through the whitening of culture and art.[23] The US mobilization of black aesthetic warfare (the use of art as a means of fighting white supremacy), in the 1960s, made the United States supplant England as the ANC's preferred site for relocation of exiles outside of Africa. During Kgositsile's exile, he was a committed member of the New York City Black Arts movement.[24] In 1962, when he arrived in New York, a reunion with the South African musician Hugh Masekela (who also left South Africa shortly after the Sharpeville massacre) led to his first introductions to many of the writers who are later at the core of the New York Black Arts movement.[25] He met LeRoi Jones before Jones moved from Greenwich Village to Harlem and redefined himself as a Black Nationalist. As Jones made the transition from his Beat period to his Black Nationalist period, Kgositsile made the transition into his new identity as a South African/ Black Arts poet. His poetry was anthologized in the most acclaimed Black Arts movement anthology *Black Fire* (1968), edited by LeRoi Jones (Amiri Baraka) and Larry Neal, and published by the major Black Arts presses (Broadside and Third World Press). During the 1970s, Kgositsile edited an anthology that combined his Black Arts poetry and the poetry of other African writers. In the 1990s, he began the production of texts that combine his Black Arts poetry and his South African-inflected poetry. During and after the 1960s and 1970s, he reframes his Black arts poetry (mixing his Black Arts poetry with his South-African inflected poetry and poetry by other African writers) until it becomes a poetics of diasporic motion.

In a 1996 interview, Kgositsile explains the movement of African American literature through South Africa. He tells a story about the circulation, throughout South Africa, of one copy of *Black Boy*. He muses:

> In the 1950's a Black sailor from the United States came to Capetown and gave someone there a copy of Richard Wright's *Black Boy*. That single copy traveled around the whole country. Each person would keep it for a week or two, read and reread it, and then pass it on. [...] Young people in South Africa were forced to be socially conscious from an early age. The ANC was everywhere. [...] I read as much as possible before I came to the United States in the 1960's. For example, I knew Leroi Jones and Ted Jones as a part of the Beat Generation. So when I met them I knew what they had written and published."[26]

This story testifies to the role of African American literature in Kgositsile's political awakening *before* he came to the United States. The story of his Black Arts Movement involvement is not the story of one text circulating, but rather the story of one person moving across the borders of African and African American poetics. He ends this story of *Black Boy* with the insistence "Bigger Thomas [the protagonist of *Native Son*] did not belong to a movement" (37). Similarly, Kgositsile's position as a South African

Black Arts poet complicates any quick and easy sense of who belonged to the Black Arts Movement.

In his third Black Arts poetry collection, *My Name is Afrika* (1971), Kgositsile reshapes Countee Cullen's famous Harlem Renaissance lyric, "What is Africa to Me?", into an even more layered inquiry: what is Africa to the black South African who, upon exile, walks into the heart of an African American love affair with a metaphor and a long-lost heritage they call "Africa"? By entitling this volume "My Name is Afrika," he claimed the name of the entire continent, at the same time as other African American Black Arts poets sought bold names that would cancel out their "slave names" from among the fragments of their knowledge of African languages. As LeRoi Jones became Amiri Baraka, Don L. Lee became Haki Madhubuti, Larry Neal remained Larry Neal, Rolland Snellings became Askia Touré, and Paulette Williams (the self-proclaimed "daughter" of the Black Arts movement – "even though they didn't know they were going to have a girl!") became Ntozake Shange, Kgositsile seems to shout, with perhaps both excitement and some bewilderment over these appropriations: "I was born on the ground you claim."[27] In a poem entitled "To Keorapetse Kgositsile" in Gwendolyn Brooks' introduction to *My Name is Afrika* (1971), she writes, "MY NAME IS AFRIKA"! / –Well, every fella's a Foreign Country. / This Foreign Country speaks to You." When African American Black Arts poets claim that they are a foreign country (Africa), Brooks' idea that everyone is a foreign country gains another dimension. "Africa," in the African American imagination, is that liberating mental space where Black Arts poets travel to decolonize their minds. In the US Black Arts movement, the term "African" had both a cultural and racial specificity. Whiteness, for example, was, by definition, not "African." In the introduction to Gwendolyn Brooks' autobiography *Report from Part One* (1972), Haki Madhubuti, one of the most influential Black Arts poets, poses the question, "Why does she call herself African?"[28] His ultimate answer becomes, "Almost for the same reason that Europeans call themselves Europeans, that Chinese call themselves Chinese, that Russians call themselves Russians, that Americans call themselves Americans" (28).

What is African American Literature?

The African-ness of Brooks is, for Madhubuti, the real name that she discovers when she purges herself of the "slave" names forced upon African Americans.

There is a call and response between Brooks' poetry and Kgositsile's. In the poem "Exile" (1975), in which Kgositsile cites some of the words in Gwendolyn Brooks' poem "Kitchenette Building" (1945), he begins with the note of the Middle Passage: "And the ocean, my brother knows, is not our friend."[29] Whereas Brooks' poem ends with an image of the shared bathrooms in kitchenette buildings and the lack of enough "lukewarm water," Kgositsile, in his response to this poem, begins with the terror of the water during the Middle Passage. After this invocation of the Middle Passage, Kgositsile moves, in the next stanza, to the need for a "community alarm" that would resound throughout the "oceans." This notion of an oceanic "community alarm" fully signals that Kgositsile envisions a "wake up" call that would be local and cosmopolitan. As he includes Brooks' words "We are things of dry hours and the involuntary plan," the oceanic "community alarm" becomes that which would awaken those who have been "grayed" by the "involuntary plan."[30] He depicts this "plan" as colonialism when he writes, "Did you say independence?" and "Lumumba, do you hear us?" (49). Brooks depicts this plan as the economic and psychological shackles that continue, in the post-slavery, post-Great Migration landscape, to reduce African Americans to "things." As Kgositsile responds to Brooks' poem, he insists on the intersections between the plan of the Middle Passage, the Black Belt neighborhoods in Chicago, and colonialism in Africa.

Kgositsile's reshaping of "Kitchenette Building" into "Exile" demonstrates his desire to add a diasporic dimension to African American poetry even as he appreciates the local specificity of this poetry. Just as Brooks sets up a phenomenology of space and sound as she wonders if "giddy sounds" like "Dream" can survive in the oppressive structure of the kitchenette buildings, Kgositsile, in the penultimate stanza, sets up a phenomenology of space and sound. He writes, "I stand among my silences/ in search of a song to lean on" (49). Just as Brooks' tenants of the kitchenette building yearn for "giddy sounds" in the harsh hall of sound "strong/ Like 'rent,' 'feeding a wife,' 'satisfying a man,'" the speaker, in "Exile," navigates an oppressive space while yearning for a redemptive sound, "a song to lean on." In "Renaissance" (2002), he advocates "breaking through the walls of our exiles" (101). As he allows the "oceanic" to penetrate the walls of Brooks' kitchenette building, he calls, in "Exile," for a common *living* room for different exiles, a space with "songs [that] will move them from our deadness" (50).

In 1973, as Kgositsile edits *The Word is Here*, he creates an anthology of modern African poetry that "break[s] through the walls of [...] exiles."[31] This anthology of poetry from across the African continent is published two years before he returns to Africa. It is divided into the following sections: "From the North," "From the East," "From the South," "From the Center," and "From the West." Comparing the poetry in these different sections and Kgositsile's Black Arts movement poetry (some of which is included in this anthology) demonstrates that Kgositsile was consciously breaking the boundaries between his Black Arts poems and African poetry.[32] He wanted his Black Arts poetry to be situated in African literary traditions.

The poems in *The Word is Here* depicting the colonized mind beg to be compared to Black Arts poetry depicting self-hatred resulting from American slavery and its aftermath. The Ugandan poet Okot p'Bitek, one of the poets in *The Word is Here*, offers a particularly vivid representation of the colonization of the mind. In the poem "My Husband's House is a Dark Forest of Books," the speaker proclaims:

> My husband has read much,
> He has read extensively and deeply,
> He has read among white men
> And he is clever like white men
> And the reading
> Has killed my man,
> In the ways of his people
> He has become
> A stump.[33]

What is African American Literature?

In the typical Black Arts poetic imagination, a similar death occurs when black people internalize antiblack racism. The idea that "the reading/ Has killed my man" is strikingly similar to the question posed in Amiri Baraka's poem "Poem for Half White College Students" (1969): "How do you sound, your words, are they/ yours?"[34] In these poems, p'Bitek and Baraka urge readers to see the colonizing mission of white-dominated educational structures. This poem "My Husband's House is a Dark Forest of Books" is first published in *Song of Lawino* (1966), p'Bitek's most acclaimed volume of poetry. At the same time as the US Black Arts movement was defining a black aesthetic as an *African* aesthetic, p'Bitek and other African poets, without Kgositsile's direct contact with the US Black Arts movement, were also reclaiming "African" as an aesthetic that can crush white power.[35]

As he anthologized the poems in *The Word is Here* (1973), Kgositsile created both these vital points of connection between his own South African/ Black Arts poetics and p'Bitek's Ugandan poetics of black-consciousness as well as points of difference between the US Black Arts ethos and 1960s and 70s African poetics. One of the poems included in the "From the East" section of *The Word is Here* begs to be contrasted with Black Arts poems, such as Haki Madhubuti's "We're an Africanpeople" (1969), that conflate the words "African" and "Black." In the poem "The Dry Well," the Ethiopian poet Solomon Deressa tells a story about "an old woman" who kills a "big lethargic black snake" on the verge of harming a three-year old child in her care. The poem ends with words "[I]t is hardly likely that she thought herself a black woman. She had no information on other pigments" (30). This African woman who does not consider herself "Black" defies Madhubuti's emphasis, in "We're an Africanpeople," on the "burning black" nature of "Africanpeople."[36] In this poem, the *fire* of blackness is the force that melds the words "African" and "people" as Madhubuti, with the loss of the space between the words, makes "African" a noun and an essence.

The Ghanaian writer Kofi Awoonor, one of the poets included in *The Word is Here*, offers, in a 1971 interview, a vehement critique of the US Black Arts poets. As Awoonor critiques Black Arts poetry, he responds to an interviewer's question "Do you feel it is always a good idea for a writer to go abroad?"[37] He states:

> It is possible to exist within your own country and still go into exile. By exile I mean distancing yourself away from those things that touch you every day, to be able to create out of them a work of art. It sounds terribly selfish not to confirm to an orthodox view of political commitment, but I believe that there is an aestheticism in a work of art. Its beauty is something we will have to take for granted. This is why I disagree with a lot of Black American poetry today. The facility of hate as embodied in "You motherfucker, stand in the corner," I do not regard as poetry. I see this as a pure splash of hate on the paper.
>
> (23-24)

When Kgositsile includes, in *The Word is Here*, both his own Black Arts poetry and Awoonor's poetry, he breaks the boundaries between that which Awoonor imagines as the Black Arts "pure splash of hate" versus the more "distanced" work of art. Unlike Awoonor, Kgositsile explains his understanding of the black aesthetic and the political in the following manner: "In a situation of oppression, there are no choices beyond didactic writing: either you are a tool of oppression or an instrument of liberation. It's that simple."[38] As Kgositsile expresses his understanding of art and protest in his poem "Notes from No Sanctuary" (1975), he insists on the power of the very words that Awoonor uses to characterize what he views as the crude didacticism of the Black Arts movement. The poem includes the question: "Where then is/ the authentic song? The determined/ upagainstthewallmothafucka act" (53). Through the lens of this poem "Notes from No Sanctuary," Awoonor's critique of Black Arts poetry is a crude reduction of the "authentic song" (the twisting of the real words into a parody).

The "real words" are the very words that Gwendolyn Brooks remembers creating such a stir when Amiri Baraka first arrives at the pivotal 1967 Black Arts Fisk University conference. In *Report from Part One* (1972), Brooks recounts:

> Up against the wall, white man! was the substance of the Baraka shout, at the evening reading he shared with fierce Ron Milner among intoxicating drum-beats, heady incense and organic underhumming. Up against the wall! And a pensive (until that moment) white man of thirty or thirty three abruptly shot himself into the heavy air, screaming "Yeah! *Yeah!* Up against the wall, Brother! KILL 'EM ALL! KILL 'EM *ALL*! I thought that was interesting. (85)

The "white man's" ability to relate to the shout "Up against the wall, white man!" signals that the Black Arts movement attacked the ideology of whiteness and white supremacy as opposed to biological whiteness. Kgositsile continues to wonder about the authentic "upagainstthewallmothafucka act" when these words in the Black Arts poem "Notes from No Sanctuary" are included in the South African anthology *If I Could Sing* (2002).[39]

In *If I Could Sing*, Kgositsile creates the South African/ Black Arts interface through the seamless mixture of the poetry written during his exile in the United States and the ones written when he returns to South Africa in 1990. He himself selects and arranges the poems. This volume begins with the nexus of "specific laughter," ghosts, and "constant beginnings," in his Black Arts poem "Origins," first published in 1970, and ends with a new poem "Rejoice" that expands the trope of naming and misnaming at the core of the Black Arts movement. These poems that begin and end the volume reveal that the Black Arts movement was one of his points of departure as he began his work as a poet but it also a part of the horizon that continues to shape the flow of his poetry. In *To the Bitter End* (Third World Press, 1995), he places South African-inflected poems within the structures that defined the Black Arts movement.[40] One of these structures is the press itself – the publication of these poems by one of the lasting institutions created during the Black Arts movement. Another structure is Black Arts rhetoric, the use of the tropes that galvanized the Black Arts movement.

Shiver: *The Diasporic Shock of Elsewhere*

In the poem "What Time is It?," one of the first poems in *To the Bitter End*, Kgositsile reshapes the trope of "nation time" into a post-apartheid issue. In Baraka's signature Black Arts poem "It's Nation Time" (1970), he captures musical, elongated sound in the words "It's nation time eye ime/ It's nation ti eye ime" (242). In "What Time is It?" Kgositsile answers with a meditation on returning home after exile. The speaker insists, "I am the man on his way home/ if peace is exile/ if peace is moving north and north/ we do not want peace" (76). This poem is dedicated to the 77th anniversary of the ANC. Nation time, in this post-Black Arts poem, becomes exiles' reclamation of lost land as the home that "is in the furnace of the womb of my eye" (76). Baraka, in "It's Nation Time," uses the word "eye" for its elongated sound and the emphasis on new ways of seeing as a core part of nation-building. Kgositsile's response references home as the "womb of my eye" and evokes the interiority of the nation that Baraka hails. This post-Black Arts poem figures "Nation Time" as "time to return home."

In 1975, Kgositsile left the United States and moved to Dar Es Salaam (where he first lived after leaving South Africa in 1961). In the 1970s, Dar Es Salaam was a hub for radical black writers and leaders and pan-African thought. As he renewed his connections to the ANC, he became, in 1983, one of the co-founders of the ANC Department of Art and Culture. "What Time is It?" in *To The Bitter End*, is published after Kgositsile's homecoming, in 1990, in South Africa. The volume is also his homecoming to Third World Press as he returns to the press that published his Black Arts volumes *For Melba* (1970) and *The Present is a Dangerous Place to Live* (1975). As he publishes three books with Third World Press (Chicago) in the 1990's, he remains very tied to his Black Arts immersion. In the 1971 introductory essay to *Directionscore: Selected and New Poems*, Haki Madhubuti asserts that African American nationalism "means publishing our own books" (21). As Kgositsile decides to publish, in the post-Black Arts movement period, with both Madhubuti's Third World Press and the two South African presses (Kwela and COSAW), he continues his commitment to the institutions created during the Black Arts movement even as his work gains the specifically South African texture that enables him to become the Poet Laureate.

In "I AM," a poem in *To the Bitter End*, Kgositsile declares himself a South African poet ("I could be that crazy/ little South African poet") even as this poem becomes a list of many different identifications that must all coexist. He connects the self-naming of 1960s Black consciousness-raising (the "I am" declarations) and the speculative next step after this consciousness-raising (the "I could be" declaration). As he uses the name "Willie" (his name often used by those closest to him), he experiments with different self-definitions including "I could be that crazy/little South African poet who insists/that the heights or flights of/artistic exploration/or the depths that any/artistic expression/might plunge into must/be dialectically related to/social relevance" (80). Through this litany of what he *could* be, the speaker in this poem makes the sheer possibilities of the "crazy little South African poet" the most alluring option. When this poem and other poems, in *To the Bitter End* (1995), are anthologized in *If I Could Sing* (2002), there is no section break between these South Africa-inflected poems and the Black Arts poems. Kgositsile's own selection and arrangement of the poems in this anthology give a metanarrative dimension to a question posed in one of the anthology's poems: "Where would any naming of this new arrangement come from" (86). The "new arrangement" of the Black Arts poems and the later poems cannot be easily "named" as African American literature versus African literature.

This question appears in the poem "Even Skin Disappears" which captures the full story he aims to tell about a non-romantic diasporic collective memory and the reasons why, contrary to what is normally assumed, it may not always be productive to simply differentiate between people's historical trauma. Evoking a Middle Passage that could be any and every diasporic trauma that has rendered subjects *black and blue*, he writes:

Shiver: *The Diasporic Shock of Elsewhere*

> Where no part of the body
> Is recognisable from any other
> Here boundaries between two people
> Disappear. Even skin
> As everything else disappears
> Even thought takes leave of absence
> There are no separate identities here
> The sword in the ceiling of her thigh disappears
> Language itself rendered speechless disappears
> Where would any naming of this new arrangement
> come from (86)

Kgositsile moves to a collective wound that makes "skin disappear"; he provides a profound lens through which to understand the role of the word "Black" in the consciousness-raising movements throughout the diaspora. Unspeakable and unnamable trauma creates the force of the name "Black."

"Even Skin Disappears" depicts the trauma that has unified people in such a violent way, whereas his poem "When Brown is Black" (1969) testifies that the word "Black" names a "new arrangement" and offers a way of reclaiming the undifferentiated, collective state as a source of power and resistance. The speaker locates a trauma that ranges "from Sharpeville to Watts / and all points white of the memory" (77). "When Brown is Black" is one of the first poems in *If I Could Sing*. As Kgositsile arranges the old and new poems in this contemporary anthology of his work, he sets up an opening and final focus on the cultural and political valence of the term "black." One of the final poems "Venceremos" expands "When Brown is Black" into an even more pointed reclamation of "black" as a unifying term that can mobilize diasporic resistance "from Sharpeville to Watts/ and all points white of the memory" (17).

"Venceremos" (2002) is a tribute to Toni Morrison's *Paradise* (1997). The race of Consolata, in Morrison's *Paradise*, is never specified but Morrison does tell readers that she is "certainly not white" (223). Through a sound "sha sha sha/ sha sha sha," she bonds with the

What is African American Literature?

"blue black" people in the all-black town Ruby, Oklahoma. The body movements and the sounds of the people of Ruby trigger the childhood memory of the city in which she lived until she was nine. The connection she makes between the people of Ruby and the people of the remembered place stems from the similar ways in which the people move. She sees both the residents of Ruby and the people in her hometown as "black," but, as Kgositsile explains, in this poetic tribute to this novel, "I love you you are mine/Must mean fellow traveler" (97). The poem's title "Venceremos" ("we shall/will defeat them") signals that Kgositsile heralds protest movements created by "fellow" travelers.[41] During the Black Arts movement, he and African American Black Arts poets became fellow travelers in the process of *shivering* toward black consciousness.

By virtue of his lived experience in both South Africa and the United States, Kgositsile gained the desire to write about a collective trauma that cannot be reduced to one geographical location. Again and again, he hits the note of the "music in the memory pried/ Open to the bone of feeling, no distances."[42] Even as scholars argue for the need for specificity in order to avoid facile conflations in studies of the black diaspora, Kgositsile calls for a recognition of the "memory pried/ Open" in African American post-slavery trauma, the post-colonial trauma he anthologizes in *The Word is Here*, and the trauma of apartheid. In "For Eusi, Ayi Kwei and Gwen Brooks," in *My Name is Afrika*, Kgositsile describes the coming together of his own travel and that of the African American Black Arts poets as the, "mov[ing] from origin to roots" (73). These words capture reconfigured diasporic connections that emerge in Kgositsile's relation to the Black Arts movement. "Origin" and "roots" are no longer the same. An "origin" is a static starting point. "Roots" are created as African American Black Arts poets mentally travel to Africa and as Kgositsile accompanies the American poets on these journeys, even as he continues to discover how his own roots in New York relate to his roots in South Africa.

Kgositsile's "practice of diaspora" includes his use of a wide range of publishing presses as he creates his transnational poetics. The

Shiver: *The Diasporic Shock of Elsewhere*

"practice of diaspora" becomes the practice of framing his poetry in the different presses that have particular centers. During his 1962–1975 sojourn in the United States, Kgositsile published with Black Arts presses (Broadside Press and Third World Press) and a larger press (Doubleday). During the post-1975 period, he published with Kwela Books (Roggebaai and Plumstead, South Africa), COSAW (Johannesburg), Achebe Publications (San Francisco), Writers' Bookmachine (Stockholm), and Third World Press (Chicago). Publishing three books with Third World Press (Chicago) in the 1990s, he remained very tied to this African American press with Black Arts origins, even as he began publishing with the non-American presses.

Although his exile from South Africa ended in 1990, until 2001 he lived half of a year in the United States and the other half in South Africa. In 2006, Kgositsile was named the Poet Laureate of South Africa. The nature of the Poet Laureate might frame him as a national icon, a poet who now clearly situates his work as "South African." In the Poet Laureate inauguration ceremony, however, his Black Arts period continues to matter. Z. Pallo Jordan, the Minister of Arts and Culture, described Kgositsile's Black Arts movement years as the "niche" he discovered in exile, the "niche" that redeemed the exile. Jordan states:

> Kgositsile found a niche among a throng of African-American literary and cultural figures who were wrestling with the strategic and aesthetic dilemmas thrown up by the struggles raging all around us in the Americas and the third world. Among them were figures such as the poet and critic, LeRoi Jones, who later took the name Amiri Baraka; the cultural activist, Norman Kelley; the writer, Lawrence Neal; the jazz aficionado and historian, A.B. Spellman and many others. It was in that literary milieu that the poet who had been struggling to come out first showed his head.[43]

The Black Arts movement is represented as Kgositsile's birth canal. Jordan's language matches Kgositsile's explanation, in a 1978 interview with Charles Rowell, that he had not written any poetry before his years in New York and that the "atmosphere" in New York was the real impetus of his first poems.[44] In "Even Skin Disappears" (1995), Kgositsile depicts a metaphoric middle passage that cannot be read as just a metaphor. He opens up the idea of *middle passages* even as the poem forces readers to think specifically about enslaved Africans on transatlantic ships. He insists that the ongoing black diasporic travel must be acknowledged without displacing the unredeemable forced movement of the Middle Passage. In "Exile," this unredeemable Middle Passage is an exile that remains unnamable. After the opening reference to the "ocean" that "is not our friend," he writes, "I wonder if our ancestors might also be/ in exile in places I dare not call by name" (49). Glissant's drawing, in *Poetics of Relation*, of the Middle Passage as a fibril, a delicate thread, connecting "African countries to the East" and "the lands of America to the West," is literally the subtextual (footnote) moment when he decides that he must move from what is unspeakable about the Middle Passage to a childlike, bare sketch that could be a Rorschach response to a therapist's questions.[45] As Glissant thinks about the problems of "root-based" identity, he hails the shiver of the rhizome identity, the "enmeshed root system," not a "totalitarian root" (11). The rhizome and rooted errantry are exemplified in the "African and American" *shivers* of Keorapetse Kgositsile.

Notes

1   Valerie Boyd, "A Protofeminist Postcard from Haiti," https://www.zoranealehurston.com/resource/a-protofeminist-postcard-from-haiti/
2   Ibid.
3   Edouard Glissant, *Poetics of Relation,* trans. Betsy Wing (Ann Arbor: University of Michigan Press, 1997 [1990]), 29–30.
4   Edwidge Danticat, "Foreword" in *Their Eyes Were Watching God*, Zora Neale Hurston (New York: Harper Perennial, 2006 [1937]), xiii.
5   Amiri Baraka, *Home: Social Essays* (New York: Akashic Books, 2009 [1966]), 104.

6   Chimamanda Ngozi Adichie, *Americanah* (New York: Anchor Books, 2013), 273.
7   Taiye Selasi, "Bye-Bye Barbar," *Callaloo*, vol. 36 no. 3, 2013, 529.
8   Darwin T. Turner, ed. *The Wayward and the Seeking: A Collection of Writings by Jean Toomer* (Washington., D.C.: Howard University Press, 1982), 123.
9   Amiri Baraka [LeRoi Jones], *Blues People: Negro Music in White America* (New York: William Morrow, Inc., 1999 [1963]), 95.
10 Chimamanda Ngozi Adichie, *The Thing Around Your Neck* (New York: Anchor Books, 2009), 144.
11 Ama Ata Aidoo, *Our Sister Killjoy: Or Reflections from a Black-eyed Squint* (Edinburgh Gate: Pearson, 1977), 61.
12 Ama Ata Aidoo, *Our Sister Killjoy: Or Reflections from a Black-eyed Squint* (Edinburgh Gate: Pearson, 1977), 3–6.
13 Ama Ata Aidoo, *The Dilemma of a Ghost and Anowa* (New York: Longman Publishing Group, 1985 [1965]), 50.
14 Zadie Smith, *Swing Time* (New York: Penguin, 2016), 215.
15 Dionne Brand, *A Map to the Door of No Return: Notes to Belonging* (Toronto: Vintage Canada, 2001), 26.
16 Michelle Wright, *Physics of Blackness: Beyond the Middle Passage Epistemology* (Minneapolis: University of Minnesota, 2015)
17 Nadia Ellis, *Territories of the Soul: Queered Belonging in the Black Diaspora* (Durham: Duke University, 2015), 4.
18 Lucille Clifton, *Blessing the Boats: New and Selected Poems 1988–2000* (Rochester, NY: BOA Editions, Ltd., 2000), 25.
19 David Chioni Moore, ed., "The Bessie Head—Langston Hughes Correspondence, 1960–1961," *Research in African Literatures*, Vol. 41, No. 3 (Fall 2010), 10, 11.
20 Langston Hughes and Arna Bontemps, ed. *The Poetry of the Negro 1746–1949* (Garden City, New York: Doubleday & Company, Inc., 1949)
21 Langston Hughes, *An African Treasury* (New York: Crown Publishers, Inc., 1960), ix.
22 Stéphane Robolin's *Grounds of Engagement: Apartheid-Era African–American and South African Writing* (2015) includes a ground-breaking study of Kgositsile.
23 The Sharpeville massacre occurred on March 21, 1960. South African police 69 black protesters (the official number). Many more people were injured.

What is African American Literature?

24 He studies briefly at Lincoln University in Pennsylvania, the University of New Hampshire, and the New School for Social Research, before he begins the Master of Fine Arts program in creative writing at Columbia University.

25 In a 1978 interview with Charles Rowell, Kgositsile explains the significance of this reunion with a childhood friend who introduced him to the emergent black aesthetic circles in New York. He states, "When I came here, Masekela and Gwangwa, a trombone player who used to play with Masekela's band, were living in New York. We had all grown up together in South Africa. Through them and a number of friendships they had established, I met a whole lot of young writers who were then living in New York. Baraka, who was then LeRoi Jones, A.B. Spellman, David Henderson, Ishmael Reed, Askia, who was then Rolland Snellings, Barbara Simmons—I met many people like those. In no time I was practically at home with them a few months after my arrival in this country—i.e., at home as far as the black community, black writers, and black musicians" (29). [Charles Rowell, "'With Bloodstains to Testify': An Interview with Keorapetse Kgositsile." *Callaloo*, No. 2 (Feb., 1978): 29]

26 Danille Taylor-Guthrie, "Conversations with South African Poet Keorapetse Kgositsile," *Issue: A Journal of Opinion (African Diaspora Studies)*, Vol. 24, No. 2: 36.

27 Ntozake Shange means "she who comes with her own things" and "she who walks like a lion" in Xhosa, the Zulu language. Shange insists, "I am a daughter of the Black Arts movement (even though they didn't know they were going to have a girl!)." This commentary is cited in: Alan Read, ed. *The Fact of Blackness, Frantz Fanon and Visual Representation* (Seattle: Bay Press, Institute of Contemporary Arts, and Institute of International Visual Arts, 1996), 159.

28 Gwendolyn Brooks, *Report from Part One* (Detroit: Broadside Press, 1972), 27.

29 Keorapetse Kgositsile, *If I Could Sing: Selected Poems* (Roggebaai, South Africa: Kwela, 2002), 49.

30 Gwendolyn Brooks, *Blacks (*Chicago: Third World Press, 1987), 20.

31 In "Dumalisile" (1995), he depicts his exile from South Africa as the attempt to silence him (to deaden his song). He writes, 'They tried to remove me from speech/ they tried to exile me to silence/ but my song elegant as the rainbow/ thunders on a clear day" (*If I Could Sing*, 77).

Shiver: *The Diasporic Shock of Elsewhere*

32 The following Black Arts poems, originally published in *For Melba* (Third World Press, 1970) and *My Name is Afrika* (Doubleday, 1971), are included in *The Word is Here*: "Origins," "Tropics," "For Melba," "For Ipeleng," "To Mother," "For Eusi, Ayi Kwei & Gwen Brooks," and "The New Breed."

33 Keorapetse Kgositsile, ed. *The Word is Here: Poetry from Modern Africa* (New York: Doubleday, 1973), 35–36.

34 William J. Harris, ed. *The LeRoi Jones/ Amiri Baraka Reader* (New York: Thunder's Mouth Press, 1991), 220–221.

35 Just as US Black Arts male poets often depict the performance of whiteness as the self-hatred stemming from the emasculation of black men by white supremacy, the speaker in "My Husband's House is a Dark Forest of Books" insists, "My husband has become a woman!" (41). These words are strikingly similar to the critique of the "deranged imitators," in Welton Smith's "Special Section for the Niggas on the Lower Eastside or: Invert the Divisor and Multiply," in *Black Fire*: "you don't just want a white woman/ you want to be a white woman" (288).

36 Don L. Lee (Haki Madhubuti), *Directionscore: Selected and New Poems* (Detroit: Broadside Press, 1971), 165.

37 Bernth Lindfors, ed. *Africa Talks Back: Interviews with Anglophone African Authors* (Trenton, N.J. & Asmara, Eritrea: Africa World Press, Inc., 2002), 23.

38 Leon de Kock, Louise Bethlehem, and Sonja Laden, ed. *South Africa in the Global Imaginary* (Pretoria: University of South Africa Press, 2004), 95.

39 The poem "Notes from No Sanctuary" is originally published, by Third World Press, in *The Present is a Dangerous Place to Live* (1975).

40 *To the Bitter End*, a volume of Kgositsile's poetry, is published in 1995 by this Chicago-based press with Black Arts movement origins and Madhubuti as the founder and ongoing director.

41 The slogan "Venceremos!" evokes social movements. The word itself is the second person plural of the future of the verb "vencer" which means "to defeat." The literal meaning is "we shall/will defeat [them]."

42 Keorapetse Kgositsile, *If I Could Sing: Selected Poems* (Cape Town, Kwela, 2002), 37. (These words appear in the poem "Point of Departure: Fire Dance Fire Song.")

43 This inauguration speech has been published at http://www.dac.gov.za/speeches/minister/Speech8Dec06.html.

44 He states, "[A]lthough I was writing before I came to this country, I had never attempted to write poetry. I was afraid. [...] [B]ut the atmosphere in New York was very good. When I first started writing poetry, I was not consciously thinking about it—this was maybe 1963 or 1964. One night before I had even thought about it, I had written a short poem which I believe is included in *For Melba*." [Charles Rowell, "'With Bloodstains to Testify': An Interview with Keorapetse Kgositsile." *Callaloo*, No. 2 (Feb., 1978): 29.]

45 Edouard Glissant, *Poetics of Relation*, trans. Betsy Wing. (Ann Arbor: University of Michigan Press, 1997 [1990]), 5.

5

Twitch *or* Wink: The Literary *Afterlife of the Afterlife* of Slavery

> Yet the difference, however unphotographable, between a twitch and a wink is vast; as anyone unfortunate enough to have had the first taken for the second knows.
> —Clifford Geertz, *The Interpretation of Cultures*

As we try to understand the continued omnipresence of the theme of slavery in African American literature, Clifford Geertz's theory of the wink and the twitch is very helpful.[1] Writers continue to *twitch* (under the spell of the ongoing psychic hold of slavery), but they also continue to *wink* (as they gesture to the limits of making slavery the eternal pivot point of African American literature). African American literature continues to be profoundly shaped by images of slavery and the afterlife of slavery. The psychic hold of slavery continues to make writers twitch and wink, and the twitches are often inseparable from the winks.

In *None Like Us: Blackness, Belonging, Aesthetic Life,* Stephen Best critiques the "temporal collapse" that happens when "what was" is imagined as "what is" (in relation to images of slavery and the afterlife of slavery in contemporary African American literature and the treatment of the past in contemporary black studies at large).[2] In the novel *The Coming* (2015), Daniel Black avoids what

What is African American Literature?, First Edition. Margo N. Crawford.
© 2021 John Wiley & Sons, Inc. Published 2021 by John Wiley & Sons, Inc.

Best refers to as "melancholic historicism" by decentering Toni Morrison's concept of "rememory" with his focus on what is coming.[3] Sun Ra's song "It's After the End of the World" could be the soundtrack of Black's *The Coming*. Black's depiction of the Middle Passage pivots on Sun-Ra-esque afterness. Black writes, "There would be a day after today" (208). *The Coming* performs a knowing and not knowing of slavery that allows us to feel melancholic historicism gaining the new mood of afrofuturistic melancholy, a melancholy that does not collapse past and present, or see the past as something we stumble into (as depicted in Morrison's *Beloved*).[4]

In *None Like Us*, when Best argues that the spatial logic of "behind, beneath, and beyond" is a part of the collapsing of the black present and slavery, he suggests that the anxiety about the impossibility of moving "beyond slavery' and the investment in thinking that slavery is "behind" and "beneath" the black present as a type of originary trauma have made it impossible for the preposition "beside" to matter (62). Black's concept of "the coming" allows the black present to be "beside" slavery and slavery to be "beside" the black present. The two-way touching, created by this besideness, connects with Hortense Spillers' emphasis on the fact that the discourse of slavery is constantly reinvented.[5] The two-way touching of the black present and slavery opens up the impossibility of separating what we think we know about slavery from what we think we know about the black present. The concept of the *coming* of the afterlife of slavery also allows the unknowability of slavery to matter even as we acknowledge that *feeling* (like performance) is another way of knowing. *Feeling* the afterlife of slavery's *coming* is not the same as *knowing* it. Feeling slavery's *coming* does not collapse past and present; feeling slavery's *coming* allows past and present to be beside each other as we feel the possibility (or, even, the certainty) that the two spheres may be connected. Feeling certain that the black present may be overdetermined by slavery, we live in profound uncertainty, or what Frantz Fanon, in *Black Skin, White Masks*, calls "certain uncertainty" (110).

Twitch or *Wink: The Literary* Afterlife of the Afterlife *of Slavery*

The Twitch and Winks in Post-Neo-Slave Narratives

Toward the end of Toni Morrison's *A Mercy* (2008), we learn that our reading of the entire novel is a reading of writing that has been written on the walls, ceiling, and floor of a house belonging to a slaveowner. Florens' furious writing makes the interior of the house seem to explode. She writes, "These careful words, closed up and wide open, will talk to themselves. Round and round, side to side, bottom to top, top to bottom all across the room. Or. Or perhaps no. Perhaps these words need the air that is out in the world."[6] With this image, Morrison unveils the *inside turned out* architecture of the psychic hold of slavery, the fact that remembering the trauma of slavery is often inseparable from the need to twist and turn its psychic hold – the need to turn this lingering pain *inside out*. We twitch as we feel that we, like Florens's words, are "closed up and wide open" in this twenty-first century architecture of African American literature.

The notion of the inside turned out architecture of the psychic hold of slavery first gained traction in Octavia Butler's *Kindred* (1979), a novel whose contemporary meditation on the slave past is imagined through the narrative device of time travel. Toward the end of *Kindred*, an unforgettable passage provides a new grammar for how we talk about the psychic hold of slavery. As Butler imagines a black subject "being still caught somehow," in the very material, bodily effects of slavery, she writes, "something ... paint, plaster, wood—a wall. The wall of my living room. I was back at home—in my own house, in my own time. But I was still caught somehow, joined to the wall as if my arm were growing out of it—or growing into it."[7] "Growing out of it" may initially sound more liberating than "growing into it," but the protagonist's (Dana's) inability to differentiate between "growing out" and "growing into" suggests that the psychic hold of slavery makes actual escape impossible. The psychic hold of slavery has made Dana an assemblage, a mix of flesh and plaster that is "caught" between the past and the present.

What is African American Literature?

If, as Ashraf Rushdy argues, the "social logic" of the neo-slave narrative begins in the 1960s, when the psychic hold of slavery meets Black Power and the critique of William Styron's *Confessions of Nat Turner* collides with revelatory new slave historiographies, then the *post*-neo-slave narrative appears, nonlinearly, before and during the twenty-first century, when the psychic hold of slavery comes into full contact with the unknown. Texts like Morrison's *A Mercy*, Edward Jones' *The Known World* (2003), Monifa Love's *Freedom in the Dismal* (1998), and Amiri Baraka's play *The Slave* (1964) are post-neo-slave narratives because they pivot on the twitch caused by the psychic hold of that which we cannot know.

The "post" in "post-neo-slave narrative" is not a chronological distinction; it is instead a space-clearing gesture that shows a conceptual, rather than chronological, difference. If the neo-slave narrative is revisionist history, the *post-neo-slave* narrative is a move from the literary imagination that fills in the gaps (that which historians cannot know) to the refusal to fill in the gaps and a lingering in the unknown. If the neo-slave narrative builds on the form of nineteenth century slave narratives, the post-neo-slave narrative may be the narratives that stop building *on* and begin to improvise, more fully, in what *A Mercy* refers to as the "ad hoc territory" (15). In a 2008 interview, Morrison uses the word "pre-racist" as a way of describing this "ad hoc territory," the liminal racial formation that had not yet (in the late seventeenth century setting of *A Mercy*) consolidated into the "black equals slave" formation of later American slavery.[8]

If the idea of literacy as freedom is a familiar frame in the foundational studies of slave narratives, the post-neo-slave narratives put pressure on readers to gain a counter-literacy, to learn to read slavery against received epistemologies.[9] Rushdy argues that the neo-slave narrative is a move to the intersubjective, for unlike the nineteenth century slave narratives, they "undermine the coherent subject of narration by developing a series of other voices which sometimes supplement and sometimes subvert the voice of the 'original' narrator" (231). Post-neo-slave narratives, like *A Mercy*, hold onto intersubjectivity and reclaim subjectivity itself in a manner that differs from the "I write, therefore I am" formulation of many nineteenth century slave narratives. In *A Mercy*, after the blacksmith accuses Florens of losing her humanity, she responds in a manner that shows that she is indeed the subject who refuses to prove her humanity and only needs "Lina to say how to shelter in wilderness" (49).

Florens and the blacksmith's exchange reworks a well-known scene from *Beloved*, in which Paul D. tells Sethe, "you got two feet, Sethe, not four." The text then reads, "[R]ight then a forest sprang up between them; tactless and quiet."[10] In *A Mercy*, this forest is not quiet when Florens seizes her right to see herself with her own eyes, and not through the blacksmith's charge that she has become a beast-like state of wilderness. Her answer is riotous: "You say I am wilderness. I am."[11] The excessiveness of this claim to self is what we need to imagine when we try to take seriously the idea that the entire novel is what she writes on the walls of the house. Florens' embrace of her black subjectivity as wilderness is her twitch out of the psychic hold of slavery. The blacksmith tells her that she has become a slave, but her *wink* ("You say I am wilderness. I am") is her move (and Morrison's move) to space for imagining the unimaginable – the possibility of radical black freedom shaped by a present that does not have to be determined by a slave past.

The architecture of the post-neo-slave narrative is the unknowable and the uncontainable, what Baraka, in *The Slave* (1964), anticipates when the play's "old field slave" declares, "We need […] a meta-language."[12] But what kind of meta-language could allow us to hear "slave" and "free" in the same temporal and spatial order? At the end of *A Mercy*, Florens writes, "Hear me. Slave. Free. I last" (189). Morrison disrupts the naturalized "from slavery to freedom" flow of the nineteenth century narrative by making us understand, in such a visual manner, that these words "Slave" and "Free" can occupy the same temporal and spatial location. The push, in post-neo-slave narratives, against the time and space of "slavery to freedom" is a push *outside* of the discourse that makes slavery legible and a push to the *wilderness* that slavery created for enslaved subjects.

What is African American Literature?

We read the words in *A Mercy* on the page but Morrison wants us to imagine reading these words on a surface that has a material presence similar to the writing of the names of enslaved Africans on the reconstruction of a wall of a slave cabin that is a part of the Oak Alley Plantation tour in Vacherie, Louisiana. When I visited this reconstruction and saw this wall of names, I felt that the only way to begin to honor the enslaved was to slowly read every name on the list, every name of the enslaved Africans who were reduced to property on this plantation. I paused at the name "Do" on the wall of this memorial. "Do" was one of the enslaved Africans on this plantation. The name "Do," on this memorial wall, may sound like a call for action (a slaveowner's command reborn as a call for reparations). The window

Figure 8. Author's Photograph, 2014.

140

Twitch or *Wink: The Literary* Afterlife *of the Afterlife of Slavery*

in the middle of the list of names makes these names seem like a move to the interiority of slavery and, also, a way of looking outward, through the window, at what cannot be contained in any enclosed museum exhibit approach to understanding American slavery.

Although Florens' writing on the wall is not a list of names, do we read her writing as we would a memorial? Since the entire novel is, finally, her writing on the wall, are we reading a novel or writing on a wall? The key difference may be the public interiority that the writing on the wall signals. The call for public interiority is a call for a memorializing that does not reinforce the boundaries between the public and the private in a manner that caters to the private zone of the national amnesia about slavery. When, in *A Mercy*, the young Florens decides that she needs "Lina to say how to shelter in wilderness," Morrison subtly proffers a distinction between monuments that are built to control the experience of historical memory and monuments that allow people to let go of the control they think they have. The post-neo-slave narrative may offer some readers (among them, descendants of enslaved Africans) a way to "breakdown" and let go of the control we might think we have when we think about slavery. If *A Mercy* is a memorial (taking us back to the dedication of *Beloved* – to "sixty million and more"), it is a memorial "in the wilderness," a "shelter in the wilderness" (49).

In "Making the Memorial" (2000), Maya Lin analyzes her 1982 Vietnam Veterans Memorial to unveil a close relationship between books and memorials. She writes, "the memorial is analogous to a book in many ways. Note that on the right-hand panels the pages are set ragged right and on the left they are set ragged left, creating a spine at the apex as in a book. Another issue was scale; the text type is the smallest that we had come across, less than half an inch, which is unheard of in monument type sizing. What it does is create a very intimate reading in a very public space, the difference in intimacy between reading a billboard and reading a book."[13] The idea of "a very intimate reading in a very public space" captures something essential in the architecture of the post-neo-slave narratives that make public the depths of the unknowability of the psychic hold of slavery.

But post-neo-slave narratives are not memorials; they are anti-memorial experimental forms. Consider, for example, Monifa Love's epistolary novel, *Freedom in the Dismal* (1998). Formally recalling Florens' love letters that become her "letter to the world," Love's novel unfolds through a series of letters, written in 1983, that tell the story of a frustrated love affair between David, a young African American man imprisoned for 30 years and Camille, a young African American woman. Despite the contemporary setting, lists of the names of slaves and free people of color who could be "witnesses" in a "Truth Commission" that shows the horrors of slavery appear throughout the novel, in-between the letters, in an unexpected, abrupt fashion. The first list of names appears in a multi-page play within the novel, presented in different fonts and graphic layouts of the words through which (the author) Love announces the "Truth Commission." Love plays with different fonts, in these opening pages, in such a dramatic fashion that the book assumes a multimedia texture. The different fonts dramatize a collision of voices and points of views through which Love suggests that the production of a testimonial space demands a capacity for improvisation. Love's use of improvisation as a foundation for the post-neo-slave narrative approximates Morrison's notion of the "ad hoc territory."

Freedom in the Dismal begins with the following boldface poster-like statement, which establishes, in the phrase of Florens' mother, that "there is no protection."

> Your own Truth Commission.
> Lights. Cameras. Notoriety.
> Days upon days of probing our
> insides. We show our insides
> gladly. All we ask is that you not
> eat them.[14]

The "[showing of] our insides" and the awareness of the threat of being consumed by an external, commodifying force vivifies the post-neo-slave narrative's heightened awareness of the forces of commodification that can create "a slavery cultural industry" that reduces the present of black people to the past historical trauma of slavery. Like Morrison's emphasis on the "open wound that cannot heal" and the fact that "there is no protection," Monifa Love emphasizes both intersubjectivity and the threat of consumption.

Those keeping order at the truth commission claim that "everyone will be heard," but Love abruptly inserts the list of names, at unexpected moments throughout the novel and at the very end of the novel, as if to remind us that the list of witnesses is a list of those who are not speaking for themselves and a list of the layers of what cannot be known. The long lists of names of the enslaved is one way that Love signals that there is no closure to the event horizon of slavery, though there is a release in the mourning that can be experienced as each individual's name is heard. The text reads:

> *Please. All witnesses will be heard. We know many of you have been waiting a very long time. Please hold on to your numbers. Everyone will be heard.*
> 21. *Daniel, a slave*
> 22. *Moses, a slave*
> 23. *Tom, a slave*
> 24. *Jack, a slave*
> 25. *Venus, a slave*
> 26. *Wallace, a slave*
> 27. *Thomas Hatchcock, a free negro*
> 28. *Andrew, a slave*
> *[...]*
> 44. *Bing, a slave*
> 45. *Nat, a slave*
> 46. *Dred, a slave*
> 47. *Arnold Artes, a free man of color*
> 48. *Nathan, a slave*
> *[...]*
> 58. *Elizabeth Crathenton, a free woman*
> 59. *Christian, a slave*
> 60. *Exum Artist, a free man of color*
> 61. *Bird, a slave*

Interspersed throughout the text, these lists convey Love's search for an archive of traces that will not inform us, but force us to accept an unknowing. "Bird, a slave" is a witness waiting to be heard. The name itself speaks, even though what is being said remains a mystery.

Mimicking these lists that seem to never end, Love shows that the open wound of slavery has never closed. In the novel, the prison industrial complex is not just what Michelle Alexander aptly names the "New Jim Crow"; Love exposes it as the re-enslavement of those suffering most from the lack of any reparations after slavery. As Love brings prison literature and slave narratives together, she foregrounds the issue of "wilderness" in a manner that adds new dimensions to Morrison's use of "wilderness" as a way of theorizing what the afterlife of slavery really is. Love anchors the emotional weight of the novel in the swamp area called the "Dismal" where Nat Turner hid. Camille's father has heard about this swamp in the oral history passed on to him. The "Dismal" where Nat Turner hid was an unsafe haven for runaway slaves. The area was life threatening but the title of the novel "Freedom in the Dismal" signals the freedom "by any means necessary" that the "Dismal" represented. Freedom by any means necessary, "Freedom in the Dismal," is what Florens embraces when she writes, "You say I am wilderness. I am."

In Edward Jones' *The Known World* (2003), the move to the unknown wilderness of slavery takes the form of foregrounding black slaveowners and slaves owned by black masters. This twenty-first century, Pulitzer Prize winning post-neo-slave narrative was published at a time when, arguably, there is more space for African American writers to address the less known and more sensitive subjects about slavery that complicate the totalizing assumptions of black innocence and white complicity in the evil that slavery was. The architecture of turning the inside out is depicted quite literally in a passage describing Fern's (a black slaveowner's) "parlor dominated by trees, a peach and a magnolia, she and her servants had managed to domesticate."[15] The "inside out" parlor is described in the following manner: "The trees in Fern's house disoriented most people, those used to the inside always being inside and the outside always being outside."[16] As Jones imagines the life of white and *black* slaveowners, he places his post-neo-slave narrative fully in the architecture of the unknown. His inscription of the psychological dimensions of being a black slavemaster and being a black person owned and reduced to property by a black person, turns slavery inside out, making readers pause and think about the horror of a character such as Henry moving from "slavery to slave master." It is hard to read this novel and not think about the widening gap, in the twenty-first century, between the descendants of enslaved Africans who are poor and intensely disempowered and the descendants of enslaved Africans whose wealth protects them from the worse forms of antiblack racism.

The novel depicts the psychic hold of slavery most powerfully when Jones describes the pain felt by the parents of Henry, a black former slave, when he first tells them that he has bought a slave. His father, in utter bewilderment and pain, beats his grown son and tells him, "Thas how a slave feel," and his son, Henry, then breaks the stick with which his father has beaten him and says, "Thas how a master feels."[17] This emphasis on the feelings of the slaves versus the feelings of the masters is one of Jones' approaches to depicting the psychic hold of slavery. Henry's parents feel connected to the enslaved even though they themselves are no longer enslaved. Henry enjoys being the mentee of Master Robbins who owned him when he was a child; he lacks a commitment to not doing anything that contributes to other black people's oppression. Some readers may connect this generational shift and the shift that some people argue separates civil rights era and post-civil rights era notions of racial solidarity. Jones shows that the psychic hold of slavery is, sometimes, black people's commitment (or lack of commitment) to other oppressed black people.

The Known World's architecture of the unknown gains a heightened dimension when the novel creates new space for imagining how the psychic hold of slavery can also produce black suspicion of other black people. As Jones draws upon the limited historical records that prove that there were some black slaveowners, he inserts the black slaveowner characters into the twenty-first century literary tradition and adds new dimensions to the common focus, in black studies, on the divide and conquer techniques of white supremacy. As Jones leans into the unknowable, he imagines scars from "divide and conquer" that are much more than the familiar focus on the divisions between the field slaves and the house slaves. Malcolm X famously says, in his most cited speech, "And today you still have house Negroes and field Negroes. I'm a field Negro."[18] Imagine Malcolm X delivering a speech about the difference between black slaveowners and the "field negroes." *The Known World* takes us to a deeper sense of the antiblackness that black people participate in when they become a part of the white supremacist power structure.

From an alternative perspective, Jones' move to foreground black slaveowners has the potential to liberate black people from the psychic hold of slavery since, if black slaveowners existed, being black cannot, in the deeper psychological registers, equal being slave. Black people's legacy does not have to be the status of slave. Jones uses the word "legacy" in a particular passage that pivots on the "melancholy" that cancels out a black futurity that could be black prosperity, not black pain. Maude, the mother of the wife of the recently deceased Henry (the prosperous black slaveowner), tries to convince her daughter to not be so grief-stricken over her husband's death that she frees or sells the enslaved he owned and abandons the slave-owning business. She tells her daughter Caldonia, "But like your father, you have too much melancholy in your blood for your own good" (181) and, later, states, "His blood [Caldonia's brother] has even more melancholy than yours. Leave it to him and your legacy will be out the door before morning" (182-183). The homonym of mourning/morning signals how deeply invested Jones is, consciously and perhaps unconsciously, in the tension between melancholia and mourning. The melancholy is figured as the weakness that makes Caldonia unable to see the bright future she can have and the "legacy" she has inherited.

Twitch or *Wink: The Literary* Afterlife of the Afterlife *of Slavery*

But, as this kaleidoscopic novel progresses with its steady introduction of new minor characters, Jones problematizes Maude's logical rejection of slavery. The eleventh chapter diverges from the main plot to offer an illustrative account of Morris Calhenny, a white slaveowner who "suffered from a crushing melancholy" (341). Beau, an enslaved African whom Morris owns, somehow understands that this "crushing melancholy" has no remedy. He and Morris, when "boys," had been "almost as close as brothers" and their closeness is due to the fact that Beau helps Morris get through the melancholic episodes without ever questioning Morris about this pain. Jones writes, "when they, Beau and Morris, had been boys, they were almost as close as brothers, and Morris would seek out Beau when the melancholy hit because Beau never asked why he suffered like that, why Morris couldn't just get up and walk away from whatever was bothering him. Beau just stayed by his side until things got a bit better."[19] Jones crystallizes the feeling of being stuck that melancholy produces. His imagining of this meeting of the white slavemaster and Beau, in this space of melancholy, is another example of the architecture of the unknown. We cannot know Beau's inexpressible melancholy as he lives his life as a person owned by this "almost brother" whose melancholy he witnesses as he remains "by his side." Jones rechannels language that encapsulates the ethos of the post-race critique of the psychic hold of slavery – "just get up and walk away from whatever" – as he "cross-racializes the wound" (Jahan Ramazani's way of thinking about the cultural hybridity that trauma can create).[20] As Jones wrote this novel about the unknowable registers of slavery, melancholy was on his mind. He uses the word "melancholy" to think about the unknowable states of depression that may have shaped the everyday life of slavery.

The story of Morris ends with the intertwined story of Henry's father, Augustus Townsend, who is shot as he "just gets up and walks away" from the man who believes he owns him (345). Augustus is a free man whose free papers are chewed up and swallowed by a slave patroller. He is sold back into slavery but refuses to live any longer as a slave. He decides that he would rather die than live again as a slave. The story of Morris begins with the "crushing melancholy" and ends with a crushing mourning incited by the image of Augustus being shot as he simply walks away from his "master." Jones shows what happens when someone "just get[s] up and walk[s] away from whatever" (341). Being stuck in the past is debilitating but pathologizing the melancholy of the grieving leads to a misunderstanding of the psychic hold of slavery; that is, we often fail to recognize the resistance and power that have been created in the space of that which appears to only be melancholy.

Joan Anim-Addo and Maria Helena Lima, the editors of *Callaloo*'s 2017 special issue on the neo-slave narrative, argue that the "main reasons for this seemingly widespread desire to rewrite a genre that officially lost its usefulness with the abolition of slavery are to re-affirm the historical value of the original slave narrative and/or to reclaim the humanity of the enslaved by (re)imagining their subjectivity."[21] If the post-neo-slave narrative is invested, to any extent, in "reclaiming the humanity of the enslaved," the emphasis is on that which Sylvia Wynter embraces as the radical black studies shift from the project of Man to a new understanding of the human. In the post-neo-slave narrative approach to black humanity, being stuck in melancholy is not pathologized and mourning is not set apart from rage, action, and resistance.

Morrison's notion, in *A Mercy*, of being human as being wild allows us to see that black ontology is not set apart from social death; black humanity is not destroyed by slavery and its afterlife. Indeed, black resistance to slavery and its afterlife resituates the very meaning of being human as being unbound. The post-neo-slave narrative's architecture of the unknown pushes us to an understanding of ontology as inseparable, as Derrida shows in *The Specters of Marx*, from "hauntology." Colin Davis, in "Hauntology, Spectres, and Phantoms" (2005), describes Derrida's theory of hauntology in the following manner:

> For Derrida, the ghost's secret is not a puzzle to be solved; it is the structural openness or address directed towards the living by the voices of the past or the not yet formulated possibilities of the

Twitch or *Wink: The Literary* Afterlife of the Afterlife *of Slavery*

future. The secret is not unspeakable because it is taboo, but because it cannot (yet) be articulated in the languages available to us. The ghost pushes at the boundaries of language and thought.[22]

The post-neo-slave narrative impulse in Morrison's *A Mercy* is a push away from the "articulated" ghost in *Beloved* to the wilderness of the "not yet formulated possibilities of the future" that Florens represents. Florens as she carves the words on the wall of the house owned by a slaveowner is refusing to allow anyone else to be the ghostwriter of her life. As Florens emphasizes "I am," after the words "You say I am wilderness," she becomes a ghostly *ghostbuster*.

Do these ghostly ghostbusters desire an ontology that is not shaped by hauntology? Morrison's reason for not ending *A Mercy* with the voice of Florens may be very tied to her awareness that readers will barely know how to read Florens' ferocious seizure of wilderness as an alternative to the skin enclosure her mother describes. As opposed to ending with the utter mystery of Florens' unsettledness, it may indeed be more comforting to hear (as the final voice in the novel) the voice of Florens' minha mae explaining how her skin became the enclosure of the wound of race. As the mother explains that, after the Middle Passage, she was taken to Barbados and "seasoned" for slavery (the very word slaveholders used as a way of describing this pre-slavery conditioning), she describes what has now become the familiar process of "epidermalization" that the widespread use of Fanon has made a huge part of our grammar for talking about race.[23] Dreaming that she could talk to Florens, her daughter whom she has not seen for so many years, the mother says, "I was negrita. Everything. Language, dress, gods, dance, habits, decoration, song—all of it cooked together in the color of my skin. So it was as a black that I was purchased by Senhor, taken out of the cane and shipped north to his tobacco plants."[24] (194). The mother explains the cooking *in* "the color of [her] skin" after she painfully passes on the inability to heal to her daughter ("an open wound that cannot heal").

The melancholy that the mother is passing on makes Stephen Best's argument, in "On Failing to Make the Past Present," even more compelling. The full novel, *A Mercy*, does indeed "incite" mourning, as Best argues, but this mourning is produced through many melancholic moments.[25] This question of passing on melancholy, of course, keeps rechanneling Morrison's words, in *Beloved*, "this is not a story to pass on." The mother's mourning sounds so different from Florens' indignant, loud, and angry mourning. Florens' response to the "withering" created when the Widow makes her feel subhuman is a mourning that sounds different from her mother's mourning.[26] Florens' mourning sounds like Fanon's description, in *Black Skin, White Masks*, of the indignant response to being fixed by the antiblack gaze: "I was indignant. I demanded an explanation. Nothing happened. I burst apart."[27] This "bursting apart" is, finally, the deeper register of Florens' proclamation "You say I am wilderness. I am."

Thinking about the psychic hold of slavery gains even more dimensions when we zoom in on this mourning that is not always legible (that makes Florens ask the blacksmith, "can you read?"[28]). Everyday black vernacular, for example, such as "what had happened was..." sounds like melancholic language stuck on the emphatic "was" as being *stuck* becomes the very energy that pushes blackened subjects forward. The everyday black vernacular sonic architecture of "what had happened *was*" may be a turning inside out of Carolivia Herron's simple and lucid diagnosis of African American family trauma in *Thereafter Johnnie* (1991): "What happened? Slavery happened."[29] Joy Leary's use of the term "post-traumatic slave syndrome" may seem too simple a diagnosis for the psychic hold of slavery that persists in the twenty-first century, but Leary's subsequent explanation of this phrase, in a 2003 grassroots community lecture, allowed me to see "shock" as a way that people hold on, precariously, not firmly, to the horror of the present feeling, sometimes, like the slavery past.[30] She asked her potentially skeptical audience, "Was any therapy ever given to the newly freed slaves? Do you think the *shock* of being so mistreated was passed on?" Trembling hands hold on when they want to let go,

Twitch or *Wink: The Literary* Afterlife of the Afterlife *of Slavery*

not due to a pathological inability to decide to "be well," but due to the life and culture created in the *shock*, in the architecture of the unknown. As Ntozake Shange tells an interviewer, "I used to have boundaries up all the time, which is limiting. [...] I never want to feel limited. If anything is life-changjng, being the descendant of a slave is. I went into therapy ten years ago because I needed to work that out. I've gotten better. Everything about me is more fluid, much less rigid. I'm gonna do everything I can, feel everything I can, until it hurts."[31] Shange implies that, as opposed to the problem of the slavery past being treated as the black present, the real problem is a state of numbness that makes us unable to mourn what we cannot know.

The call for collective mourning in the space of the unknown sets the post-neo-slave narrative apart from the neo-slave narrative. This impulse to privilege collective unknowing as collective mourning is the mood of the post-neo-slave narrative. This mood cannot be periodized; it appears in 21st century texts such as Jones' *The Known World* and Morrison's *A Mercy and earlier African American literature*. The psychic hold of slavery creates the external, collective work of culture; the inner, psychic hold is turned inside out as the unknown becomes the strange *structure* of feeling, the *twitch*, that makes Gwendolyn Brooks write, "In the wild weed/ she is a citizen."[32]

Winking at the Psychic Hold of Slavery in Black Arts Movement-Era Drama

As the 1960s and early 1970s Black Arts Movement (BAM) called for the abandonment of "slave names" and slave mentalities, it called for a letting go of the psychic hold of slavery. BAM-era drama shows how winking about slavery's hold is performed in African American literature. The winks (the feeling that the twitch caused by the psychic hold of slavery eases into a wink) emerge as writers perform an exhaustion with the equation of slave body and black body.

Amiri Baraka coined the neologism "atmos-feeling" in the opening stage directions of *Slave Ship: A Historical Pageant* (1967). He writes: "Whole theater in darkness. Dark. For a long time. Just dark. [...] Burn incense, but make a significant, almost stifling, smell come up. [...] These smells, and cries, the slash and tear of the lash, in a total atmos-feeling, gotten some way."[33] The BAM often depicted slavery as the historical trauma that created an agonized collective black body, what Baraka calls *"pushed-together agony"* in the stage directions in *Slave Ship* (135). The movement's hailing of black love as the desire to be together is a swerve from the trauma of slavery, from the "scene of the crime" as Baraka names it in *Blues People* (95). BAM writers staged slavery as the environment that created the self-hatred that makes black people not want to be together, the environment that makes togetherness always feel forced and painful. As the movement raged against the scene of the crime and as it imagined scenes of resurrection, the performance of togetherness as black power and black feeling led to a re-envisioning of drama as "ritual," actors as "liberators" (per Barbara Ann Teer, founder of the National Black Theatre), and audience members as "participators."[34]

Baraka's atmos-feeling is intimately tied to this revisionist drama of actor–liberators and spectator–participants. In *The Drama of Nommo*, Paul Carter Harrison describes the way in which these liberators and participants co-created the event of Black Arts drama, and he uses Baraka's *Slave Ship* as a prime example of a play that affects the "entire viscera": "There was no way for us to step outside of Gil Moses's production of Imamu Baraka's *Slave Ship*. The event was suspended in time, our entire viscera responding to the urgency conjured up to survive the trip across the Middle Passage" (Harrison 35). As his atmos-feeling connects the atmospheric and the visceral, Baraka anticipates Sara Ahmed's theory of the affective energy with which people's moods and tensions shape their experience of an atmosphere. In "Atmospheric Walls" (2014), Ahmed opens up a new way of thinking about the interplay between our affective states and the atmosphere of the rooms we inhabit:

> The atmosphere is not simply "out there" before it gets "in": how we arrive, how we enter this room or that room, will affect what impressions we receive. To receive is to act. To receive an impression is to make an impression. So we may walk into the room and "feel the atmosphere," but what we may feel depends on the angle of our arrival. Or we might say that the atmosphere is already angled; it is always felt from a specific point.[35]

Ahmed's theory of atmosphere as that which is "not simply 'out there'" differs from the arguments of Christina Sharpe and others, who characterize anti-black racism – that is, the afterlife of slavery – as a type of weather or atmosphere.[36] Just as Baraka offers the neologism "atmos-feeling," Ahmed provides a new grammar that allows us to understand atmosphere's relation to the afterlife of slavery as less a sphere of inevitable influence than one in which the "angles of our arrival" recreate the afterlife of slavery, everyday, in rooms where we do not (and should not) want to live but live regardless.

Thinking about the atmos-feeling – and not the atmosphere – of the afterlife of slavery offers a way of feeling slavery's imprint on the black present without converting that feeling into a sphere of knowledge or witnessing. In *None Like Us* (2018), Stephen Best argues that collapsing the black present and slavery creates a melancholic historicism, a dead-end focus on the past, which cancels out what José Esteban Muñoz, in *Cruising Utopia,* calls the "not yet here," a queer relation to futurity that does not see the future as a reproduction of the past.[37] When Best argues that the spatial logic of "behind, beneath, and beyond" shapes the collapse of the black present and slavery, he suggests that we need the idea of besideness in order to signal the hovering effects of slavery without making what hovers into what is (62). Thinking about the besideness of slavery and the black present signals a loosening of the psychic hold of slavery. The parallel lines of slavery and the black present cannot be collapsed. The discourse of slavery, as Hortense Spillers emphasizes, is constantly reinvented.[38] If slavery is beside the black present, it is too close to be dismissed as "over" and too sideways to be the foundation of how we understand the black present. In order to experience the besideness, we have to feel the closeness of the slave past and black present and the simultaneous distance between slave past and black present. The afterlife of slavery creates the presence of the absence of slavery, what Frantz Fanon calls the "certain uncertainty."[39]

Jared Sexton's suggestion that "black life is *lived* in social *death*" synthesizes the Afro-pessimist paradigm: "Rather than approaching (the theorization of) social death and (the theorization of) social life as an 'either/or' proposition, then, why not attempt to think them as a matter of 'both/and'?"[40] But Baraka's atmos-feeling of blackness – as a resurrection of the dead, a resurrection from slavery – refuses to accept this forced, everyday relation to death. What is radical, rather, is the feeling that blackness need not always already be tied to the status of the slave or the omnipresence of death. Like Baraka's *Slave Ship*, Marvin X's play *The Resurrection of the Dead* (1969) reveals the BAM's thematization of slavery as a way of moving past the equation of blackness with death. When the play, identified as a "ritual," appeared in the journal *Black Theatre*, X included line drawings that depicted, first, a mound of bodies almost dead from the Middle Passage and, then, a procession of resurrected bodies, "standing now," who "find each other" and "sing and dance." The BAM's dramatization of slavery was overdetermined by the movement's interest in the dramatic power of the scene of black resurrection.

Best argues that the investment in slavery as the "scene of the crime" continues to reproduce an investment in a narrative of originary trauma, but Baraka, despite using the phrase in *Blues People*, never meant for blackness to be defined this way. His notion of atmos-feeling teaches us how to break out of an atmospheric swallowing up of blackness by the discourse of slavery. In its stead is a resurrected blackness that gives us the ability to imagine black life, in the present tense, as the constant, everyday, radical decentring of black death. Best begins *None Like Us* by confessing that, "for as much as attempts to root blackness in the horror of slavery feel intuitively correct, they produce in me a feeling of unease, the feeling that I am being invited to long for the return of a sociality that I never had" (1). Baraka's atmos-feeling, meanwhile, invites a communitarianism that is rooted not "in the horror of slavery" but in the resurrection from slavery. Spillers explains this bond when she writes, "I have always regarded my membership in my natal community as an ethical obligation. In brief, not to assume it, but to tend and attend it with a most careful eye" (6). Unlike Baraka and Spillers, Best cannot feel the depth of the decision, often made by the descendants of enslaved Africans, to belong to one another. But Best connects with Spillers in their shared emphasis that we cannot know slavery itself "before discourse touched it" (Spillers, "Changing" 179). And he aligns with Baraka in their mutual foregrounding of "feeling"– the atmos-feeling of resurrection for Baraka and the "feeling of unease" for Best – as they refuse to accept that slavery and its afterlife are always already the atmosphere of blackness.

The performance of atmos-feeling in Baraka's BAM plays about slavery begs to be compared to the relationship between bodies and atmosphere in Adrienne Kennedy's *Funnyhouse of a Negro* (1964) and Ntozake Shange's *For Colored Girls Who Have Considered Suicide / When the Rainbow Is Enuf* (1975). With an eye to the deeper dimensions of the differences between the twitch and the wink in response to the psychic hold of slavery, I argue that Baraka's atmos-feeling explains the rethinking, during the Black Power era, of the tension between feeling black and feeling like a slave. Slavery was reimagined in this period as the force that had to be decentered by black consciousness. The tension between the afterlife of slavery and the new life of the "negro" becoming "black" is the vibrating edge of BAM-era performances of slavery.

Baraka's Reinvention of Slavery in *Slave Ship* and *The Slave*

By insisting on the difference between Negro and Black – that is, between slave and revolutionary subject – the BAM fundamentally reinvented the discourse of slavery, maintaining that both the end and the afterlife of slavery be recognized. Baraka's *Slave Ship* was first performed by the Spirit House Movers in 1967 in Newark, New Jersey, in a production directed by the playwright. Two years later, Gilbert Moses's Off-Broadway production added congas, bass, and the trumpet to the drum and saxophone mentioned in the play's stage directions, sonic additions which honoured the sensory overload Baraka sought to achieve in his production of theatrical atmos-feeling.

Unusually, *Slave Ship*'s prop list includes "Smell effects: incense … dirt/filth smells/bodies," an atypical inclusion that emphasizes the multisensory materiality of the play's atmosphere.[41] Indeed, the note signals the flow of affective energies that shape the atmos-feeling of slavery's afterlife. Smell continues to figure prominently in the opening stage directions, which list *"Pee. Shit. Death,"* before folding the olfactory into the broader atmospheric environment of the stage picture: *"Life processes going on anyway. These smells, and cries, the slash and tear of the lash, in a total atmos-feeling, gotten some way"* (132). Baraka stages slavery as the environment that produces not death but the *"slash and tear"* that black life becomes, and rather than simply describe this feeling, Baraka aims to capture its affective and atmospheric quality in the environment of the slave ship on stage. Black feeling thus emerges as an emanation of the onstage ecology of the "slave ship," which audiences understand as an environment tied to the "voices of African slaves": the Curser, the Struggler, the Prayer, the "Screamer-Attacked," and so on (131). *Slave Ship* stages slavery as atmosphere, not event, which allows Baraka to anticipate the current discourse of the afterlife of slavery.

But the BAM's framing of slavery differs from twenty-first-century Afro-pessimism: unlike the Afro-pessimist construal of blackness as "black life […] *lived* in social *death*" (Sexton 29; emphasis in original),

Twitch or Wink: The Literary Afterlife of the Afterlife of Slavery

Slave Ship imagines blackness as the feeling that emerges *against* slavery. The stage directions indicate the "*[s]ounds of people picking up. Like dead people rising. And* against *that, the same sounds of slave ship*" (143; emphasis added). In the BAM imagination, slavery is both the atmosphere and the spatio-temporal dimension that must be pushed against. Sharpe writes, "The weather is the totality of our environments; the weather is the total climate; and that climate is anti-black" (104). But this naturalizing of anti-blackness differs from Baraka's reinvention of slavery as an atmos-feeling that must be resisted in order to create "black space." The BAM's ethos of black cultural nationalism needed too much space for agency and resistance to let slavery become the all-determining air of black experience. In *Slave Ship*, the desire to mobilize radical black nationalism pushes against any desire to reveal the horrors of slavery. In the midst of the movement's radical black nationalist mission, therefore, artists, writers, and critics centred slavery only in order to decentre it.

The sonic atmos-feeling of *Slave Ship* similarly works to dismantle the overdetermining atmosphere of slavery. The "*new-sound saxophone*" is described, in the stage directions, as "*tearing up the darkness*" (142), performing a kind of sonic warfare as the sounds that "*come up out of the actors*" blend into the soundscape of the ship (132). The stage directions' emphasis on this syncretic aurality ("*Ommmmm sound, mixed with sounds of slave ship, saxophone and drums*" [143]) signals that the chanting and humming throughout the play contribute to a meta-sonic atmosphere blending black sound and the "*killed white voice*" (145). The humming, in particular, represents the black hold – literally, the hold of the ship – that sounds "*as if it would go on forever*" (143).

While the play's opening stage directions plunge the "*[w]hole theater in darkness. Dark. For a long time. Just dark*" (132), Baraka decenters this darkness by the end of play when the slave ship becomes "*an actual party*" (145) – specifically, a dance party. If *Slave Ship* begins with people "*mashed together in common terror*" (132), forced to move collectively, it ends radically with movement, dance, and "*loose improvisation*" (145) tied to individual will. The "*pushed-together agony*" (135) of the slave ship is rechanneled at the end of the play into a shared atmosphere of pushing out together. More than any other African-American cultural movement, the BAM set in motion the concept of the black body as the black mind. Any discourse of slavery's afterlife that cancelled out the aliveness of the black body, therefore, was antithetical to the BAM's cultural nationalist investment in the black body as the most local alternative nation-state. The black body – as opposed to the negro slave body – became an anti-slavery site of resurrection.

We see the call for bodily resurrection in a production still, published in the June 1973 issue of *Black World*, from Moses's Off-Broadway production of *Slave Ship*. An actor in a white mask looks down at a slave writhing in pain at the edge of the stage, one arm pressed against his stomach and the other stretched out toward the audience. This body in pain, whose extended arm reaches past the fourth wall and breaks free from the confines of the stage, suggests a similar breaking free from stagings of slavery, gesturing toward a spatio-temporality in which the black body on stage need not be the slave body in pain. In "The Slavebody and the Blackbody," Toni Morrison muses, "The slavebody was dead, wasn't it? The blackbody was alive, wasn't it?"[42] In Moses's production of *Slave Ship*, the body at the edge of the stage speaks to the desire to lift the black body out of the ongoing re-enactment of slavery.

In Baraka's *The Slave* (1964), only the prologue – delivered by the character Walker Vessels, "*dressed as an old field slave*" – is set during slavery.[43] The start of Act One shifts to the interior of a present-day house in an unnamed city where a Black Power urban rebellion is unfolding. Walker has broken into the home of Grace, his ex-wife, a white woman who ended their marriage when he became a black nationalist and began "preaching the murder of all white people" (72). Grace's new husband, Brad Easley, is a white male professor who has always disliked Walker (even before his black nationalist stage, when Easley knew him as a young, aspiring poet). While Walker, in a drunk, violent state and wielding a gun,

158

holds the pair hostage, Easley mocks Walker's newfound black radicalism, arguing that the Black Power movement is a self-pitying form of collective narcissism and misguided violence. In Act Two, Walker kills Easley, and the explosions from the black urban riot outside cause the "white" house to begin literally falling apart, a soundscape punctuated by the cries and screams of a child. When Grace pointedly asks, "How do you know they're dead, Walker?" (88), Baraka leads us to think that Walker may have killed his and Grace's biracial daughters while in a state of hysteria that made him think he was rescuing them from white power.

When falling beams kill Grace and injure Walker, the final stage directions indicate that Walker "*stumbl[es] unsteadily through the door*" and becomes "*the old man at the beginning of the play*" (88), a looping back that makes clear Baraka's intention to bring the 1960s Black Power movement into collision with the era of slavery. In *The Slave*, slavery is a prelude: it is the frame of the frame, the edge that makes the interior drama possible. And the play's cyclical structure re-emphasizes the opening prologue delivered by the field slave, who speaks about "meta-language" and "phenomenological fields" (45) and whose contingent, fractured points of view merge the wise philosopher and the exhausted old man musing about the conundrums that have shaped his life. Baraka thus shapes the time of slavery into an atmosphere in which the deepest, most honest reflections happen. When at the end of the prologue the slave slides into his present-day iteration in the 1960s, slavery becomes again, as in *Slave Ship*, a scene of procession, the point at which the drama begins but does not remain.

When slavery overdetermines our understanding of blackness, we can't hear the sort of unnaming Baraka performs in "Something in the Way of Things (In Town)" (2002), his spoken-word collaboration with the hip-hop band The Roots. In the song, Baraka refrains from naming the afterlife of slavery as the "something" that is "in the way of things," as though he seeks to articulate a contemporary black pain that evades nomenclature: "You just can't call its name name name name name name name." The repetition of the word "name" is an echo, not the chant that shaped so many BAM poems, and thus the song allows us to re-hear the simultaneous centring and decentring of slavery that also occurs in Baraka's BAM-era plays. And just as he does in his plays, Baraka describes a multi-sensory experience: if he first "see[s] something in the way of things / Something to make us stumble / Something get us drunk from noise and addicted to sadness," sight and sound cede to a reshaping of the discourse of slavery as feeling – "I see something and feel something stalking us."[44]

This move from discourse to feeling marks the end of the prologue in *The Slave*, when Walker's voice transforms from that of the philosopher to that of the 1960s black army leader in the middle of a color-line war: "*Running down, growing anxiously less articulate, more 'field hand' sounding, blankly lyrical, shuffles slowly around, across the stage, as the lights dim and he enters the set proper and assumes the position he will have when the play starts ... still moaning*" (45). If the discourse of slavery is "*articulate*," the feeling tied to it – too slow and shuffling to be adequately named – is the "*blankly lyrical.*" For Baraka, then, the afterlife of slavery is an unnameable feeling that "stalks," to return to his collaboration with The Roots, which sheds more light on his use of the term "atmos-feeling" in *Slave Ship*. When slavery is experienced as an atmos-feeling, it is not a total environment that can be known and named. Slavery and its afterlife form part of a larger environment with too many other things in the air. It is the "something in the way of things," accessed only by language that is "blankly lyrical."

In *The Slave*, Grace accuses Walker of being riven by his conflicting feelings: "You're split so many ways ... your feelings are cut up into skinny horrible strips ... like umbrella struts ... holding up whatever bizarre black cloth you're using this performance as your self's image" (61). Later in the play, Walker tells Grace, "I hated you when I wanted you" (65). When Walker calls Easley "boss man," it is clear that slavery is one (or more than one) of the "skinny horrible strips" of feeling that hovers over this mid-1960s scene of color-line drama. As Baraka strips the discourse of slavery of its totalizing power, he invests the feeling of slavery with unknowability, a sense of the mysterious, rather than the authority of a totalizing narrative. Baraka's emphasis, in *In Our Terribleness*, on *looking* at the fact of slavery – "But look at it / We were brought here slaves and survived that / Now we are trying literally to get our selves back together" – is articulated in *The Slave* as a quieter *listening*: "But listen now ... Brown is not brown except when used as an intimate description of personal phenomenological fields. As your brown is not my brown, et cetera, that is, we need, ahem, a meta-language. We need some thing not included here. (*Spreads arms*)" (45). This reshaping of what we expect to hear from an "old field slave" is Baraka's call for a way to think about slavery that does not totalize its discourse. The meta-language Baraka advocates, therefore, is one that might teach us to hear of Walker's "personal phenomenological fields" without imagining the fields once worked by slaves.

Spillers reminds us that the discourse of slavery is always liable to reproduce a cancelling that has been naturalized since the Middle Passage: "before the 'individual,' properly speaking, with its overtones of property ownership and access, more or less complete, stands the 'one'" (395). When Spillers argues that "the one" is both a "position in discourse" and the "one in the act of speaking" (395), we see her connection with Baraka. In *The Slave*'s prologue, Walker represents both the discursive position of the "slave" and the subject speaking (himself) out from the position he has been assigned. For the BAM, slavery is a discursive relation that propels a speaking out from the naturalized discourse that turns blackness into what Spillers recognizes as the sociological mass – that is, the "posited belief that empirical data insist on" (395). For both Spillers and Baraka, the dilemma is not whether to choose between the one or the mass but rather how to cultivate a new grammar that allows us to feel the one-in-the-mass – a concept of "the one" that does not privilege individualism set apart from the black masses. Walker is "the small integrity of the now that accumulates the tense of the present as proofs of the past" (Spillers 396).

Ntozake Shange's Performance of Body/Air Tensions

The BAM's move toward what A.B. Spellman has called the "sensuality of a collective consciousness that declared itself on sight" was a move toward an atmos-feeling that could break the psychic hold of slavery by refusing to let its discursive afterlife overdetermine the black "collective."[45] In the introduction to her play *For Colored Girls Who Have Considered Suicide / When the Rainbow is Enuf*, Ntozake Shange uses the image of an "arched back over a yawn" to explain the play's investment in the sensuality of a black feminist collective consciousness, one set in motion by exhaustion and boredom with dominant ways of talking about being black and a woman.[46] She articulates this sentiment in one of the play's most cited lines: "but bein alive & bein a woman & bein colored is a metaphysical dilemma / i haven't conquered yet" (45). As Shange reinvents the discourse of black women's trauma, she finds a new grammar, through dance and the spoken word, that lets us feel the alive-ness that is constantly crushed when the slave past necessarily becomes the prism through which to understand the black present.

For Shange, the present is charged air, an atmos-feeling created as black women's bodies interact with the air and light of the environment, and the stage directions in *For Colored Girls* foreground the tension between bodies and atmosphere: for instance, "*There is a sudden light change, all of the ladies react as if they had been struck in the face*" (16), and later, "*The lights change, and the ladies are all hit by an imaginary slap, the lady in red runs off up left*" (21). Shange shapes light into a force that can strike, even as it lacks the "real" material presence of the women's bodies. The stage directions note the slap is an imaginary one – perhaps the memory of slaps that really happened, that came from hands and bodies as "real" as those of the women on stage – yet this imaginary force still commits violence and causes pain. The materiality of this imaginary slap recalls Louis Althusser's discussion of the tension between the "real" and the "imaginary" when ideology transforms individuals into subjects:

"Ideology represents the imaginary relationship of individuals to their real conditions of existence."[47] In *For Colored Girls*, the physical impact of the imaginary slap reveals the extent to which "real conditions of existence" are shaped by the power structures built around them. The play contains only one direct reference to slavery, when the lady in brown describes her childhood "love affair" with Toussaint L'Ouverture, who "led they army of zombies / walkin cannon ball shootin spirits to free Haiti / & they waznt slaves no more" (27). The reference registers Shange's defiance of an ideology that equates blackness with the feeling of a slave or ex-slave. She seeks instead an atmos-feeling that allows the pain and aftereffects of slavery – along with the host of other oppressive forces against which black women struggle – to be experienced as both the "real conditions of existence" and the "imaginary" (Althusser 109). Shange finds an opening in this atmos-feeling where the power of dominant structures collides with the power of individuals, where a discourse of always-already-free has to be felt, simultaneously, alongside the discourse of always-already-enslaved.

Shange's stage directions often call for the performers to freeze, effecting a stillness that signals the body's embeddedness in its atmosphere. The dancing body, momentarily frozen, performs atmos-feeling – that is, the mutual interaction between one's own energy and the energy of the dominant atmosphere. Shange's use of stillness in this way recalls the "arched back over a yawn" (xi). This evocative image draws our attention not only to the peculiar shape of the backward bend but also to the breath, the intake of air that loosens and curves the spine as the body settles into, and luxuriates for a moment in, the involuntary reflex. The image offers a way of understanding the stillness required by the play's choreography: when the performer freezes, she is momentarily suspended in atmos-feeling, a reciprocal relationship between body and atmosphere. She concentrates on remaining still while at once abandoning herself to the affective responses of her body to its environment.

Atmos-feeling is interrogated during the first sequence of Shange's "choreopoem," which Cheryl Clarke interprets as Shange's

What is African American Literature?

imagining of a chorus of performance poems women wrote during the BAM.[48] Seven performers take turns positioning themselves outside of particular US cities:

lady in brown	i'm outside chicago
lady in yellow	i'm outside detroit
lady in purple	i'm outside houston
lady in red	i'm outside baltimore
lady in green	i'm outside san francisco
lady in blue	i'm outside manhattan
lady in orange	i'm outside st. louis (5)

This positionality, this explicit location on the periphery, adds new dimensions to Shange's approach to atmos-feeling. Here, the feeling of being "outside" synthesizes the play's exploration of the ways in which black women are denied access, rendered something other than inhabitants of their locations. Shange thus suggests that black women are outside a legible geography, a status that shapes their interaction with legible, dominant sites; for the women in *For Colored Girls*, atmos-feeling refers to their experience of being outside the named structures and sites they are thought to inhabit.

Shange explores this notion of peripherality in her novel *Sassafrass, Cypress and Indigo* (1982) too, emphasizing the feeling of living outside of named, dominant, legible sites – both materially and psychically. A kind of refrain emerges in the novel: "the slaves who were ourselves," a phrase that connects the black present to slavery in a way that refuses to deny enslaved Africans the humanity of twentieth-century African Americans.[49] Like the women outside cities in *For Colored Girls*, "the slaves who were ourselves" in *Sassafrass* feel the afterlife of slavery by highlighting the illegible zone that falls outside of *slavery as the past*. The refrain collapses the present into the past and vice versa, an impossible temporality that becomes perhaps the only time frame that allows discourses of slavery's afterlife to lean into the inseparability of the speculative and the factual.

Twitch or *Wink: The Literary* Afterlife of the Afterlife *of Slavery*

This connection between the speculative and the historical animates the BAM's mobilization of "black" as expressly distinguished from "slave." The blackness hailed by the movement was sustained by a powerful speculative narrative of the subject resurrected from the slave condition while still committed to exposing the horrors of what Baraka called the primal "scene of the crime" that attempted to equate blackness with slavery. This narrative of resurrection from slavery might remind us of Spillers' characterization of slavery's afterlife as a "hieroglyphics of the flesh" (207), an inheritance of the historical fact that human bodies were branded during slavery, the legacy of bondage inscribed on their skin. Spillers conveys the mystery and materiality of black people's lived experiences of the afterlife of slavery. Shange, too, seeks a way of touching the mystery of slavery's afterlife without assuming she can really know it. We hear Shange's speculative dramatic impulse in *For Colored Girls*'s opening sequence, when one woman asks, "Are we ghouls?" (4). One definition of *ghoul* refers to "one who shows morbid interest in things considered shocking or repulsive" ("Ghoul"), which exposes an element of the BAM's investment in dismantling the discursive equation of blackness with slavery.[50] The BAM anticipated Afro-pessimism's "morbid interest" in social death as a way of understanding blackness. Unlike Baraka, who imagines resurrection from slavery, the BAM-era feminist work of Shange asks us to imagine enslaved Africans and their descendants as somehow outside – indeed beyond – slavery's master narrative of death and within an atmos-feeling of radical life.

Atmos-Feeling in *Funnyhouse of a Negro*

Adrienne Kennedy's *Funnyhouse of a Negro* was inspired by the playwright's travels to Africa, where she first conceived the play, and Europe, where she finished it, and the play captures the confusion and unknowability that arise when one unconsciously imports the logic of slavery's afterlife into the discourses of colonialism and decolonization.[51] Kennedy explains that, during the months she lived in Ghana, she was unable to straighten her hair for the first time (27), which explains the motif of hair – "wild" hair, hair falling out, baldness – that recurs in the play's nightmare of racial self-hatred. The play begins with a woman "*carrying before her a bald head.* [...] *Her hair is wild*" (5), and throughout the play, many of the protagonists's multiple selves (a reflection of her fractured psyche) lose their hair in handfuls. Sarah, a biracial woman whose idolization of whiteness causes her to despise her own blackness, connects this loss of hair to the hatred and revulsion she feels toward her black father, whom she claims "is the darkest of them all" (19). Thus, when "*a large dark faceless man*" enters the stage and tells us, "It begins with the disaster of my hair" (13), he crystallizes the metanarrative of racial self-hatred that structures the entire play. Kennedy connects the play's imagery to a number of the sites she visited during her travels, but she specifically mentions "Ghana, fall 1960; [...] the birth of Ghana newly freed from England" ("On the Writing" 27). *Funnyhouse* channels the angst of the "newly freed" into surreal performances of internalized anti-black racism and self-hatred – consider, for instance, how the play's use of the word *negro* signals the colonized mind trying to feel free – which brings Kennedy into alignment with the BAM's insistence on art for liberation's sake.

Kennedy, like Baraka, shaped her BAM-era drama into performances of atmos-feeling; in her plays, atmosphere is not always already "out there" but it itself the tension that emerges as individuals interact with dominant structures. Sarah's desire to gain access to whiteness coexists with her need to purge herself of the violence of anti-black racism, and thus the "funnyhouse" of her psyche becomes populated by numerous selves that see everything through the polarized logic of white and black. Kennedy makes a pointed distinction in the play between places and rooms. As Sarah states, "I know no places. That is, I cannot believe in places. To believe in places is to know hope and to know the emotion of hope is to know beauty. It links us across a horizon and connects us to the world. I find there are no places only my funnyhouse. Streets are rooms, cities are rooms, eternal rooms" (10). Since Kennedy emphasizes that *Funnyhouse* is set in Sarah's "room," she frames the play as the performance of everything that happens around its protagonist. In the author's note at the start of the text, Kennedy writes, "*Funnyhouse of a Negro* is perhaps clearest and most explicit when the play is placed in the girl Sarah's room. The center of the stage works well as her room, allowing the rest of the stage as the place for herselves. [...] When she is placed in her room with her belongings, then the director is free to let the rest of the play happen around her" (4). Sarah's room is the center of an atmosphere, a locus for the circulation of bodily, psychical, historical, and environmental energies.

The play pivots on the tension between structures and bodies. Consider the following stage direction that describes the movement of a body through walls:

> *Now the light is focused on a single white square wall that is to the Left of the Stage, that is suspended and stands alone, of about five feet in dimension and width. It stands with the narrow part facing the audience. A character steps through.* [...] *She is the Negro.* [...] *She steps slowly through the wall, stands still before it and begins her monologue*[.] (7)

During her speech, the stage directions indicate that other characters, too, "*come through the wall, disappearing off into varying directions in the darkened night of the Stage*" (9). These repeated instances of bodies moving through walls, similar to the "atmospheric walls" Sara Ahmed theorizes, convey, literally and visually, a moving through the abstract yet concrete structures that are the afterlives of slavery and colonialism. Kennedy's hailing of the character – "*She is the Negro*" (7) – depicts the consolidation of the subject position "Negro" as a process of moving through such structures. The structure does not simply produce the subject, therefore, but is rather hailed by *moving through* the structure.

Here is the difference between the "fact of blackness," Charles Lam Markmann's mistranslation of chapter five in Fanon's *Black Skin, White Masks* (82), and the "lived experience of blackness,"

Richard Philcox's more accurately translated phrase (89): where the former translation describes the production of the subject by a hegemonic power structure, the latter accounts for the black subject's power to interact with the terms of structural interpellation as she moves through the world. Fanon's work helps to shed light on the atmos-feeling of *Funnyhouse of a Negro*, given the extent to which the play stages not only the tension between individual affect and history but also the consonances between the afterlife of slavery and colonialism. Fanon too invokes the surreal afterlives of colonialism and slavery, foregrounding, like Kennedy, the funnyhouse effect of being black in an anti-black world, tellingly describing the afterlife of slavery and colonialism as "an "*atmosphere* of certain uncertainty" (*Black Skin* 90; emphasis added). This "certain uncertainty" best approximates the tenor of our endless reinventions of slavery – for we can never know what slavery really was nor what it really felt like, even as we continue to feel its effects.

Funnyhouse of a Negro pivots on the performance of this certain uncertainty, as its surreal aesthetic competes with its historical content. Kennedy dramatizes the afterlives of colonialism and slavery by imagining the degree to which Sarah's existence is caked with their residue. In Sarah's room, teeming with her multiple selves, the present does not become the past; rather, the past "*steps through*" the present (9). The encounter of past and present that marks the atmos-feeling of the play makes explicit the psychic hold of colonialism and slavery. But the play never explains the insanity it performs; its speculative atmos-feeling never settles into the fact of an atmosphere of anti-black racism created by the legacies of colonialism and slavery. By depicting the passage through porous walls as analogous to the move beyond the hold of structural forces, Kennedy resists the logic that would equate blackness with slavery, the sentiment Frank Wilderson articulates when he insists, "Blackness cannot disentangle itself from slaveness."[52]

Funnyhouse of a Negro theatrically renders what Fanon describes as a "genuine dialectic between my body and the world," exploring the discursive excesses of colonialism and anti-black racism and their impact on the "slow construction of my self as a body in the middle of a spatial and temporal world" (*Black Skin* 91). This "slow composition" articulates the everyday unsettledness of be(com)ing black, something Kennedy alludes to in the play's "*jungle*" scene, which the stage directions indicate "*is the longest Scene in the play and is played the slowest*" (21). The slow process of becoming black, for both Kennedy and Fanon, involves the terror of navigating a colonized mind that has internalized anti-black racism – but has not been colonized enough not to feel that white supremacy is absurd. Fanon's "Look! A Negro!" sequence captures the absurdity of this slow process, this interpellation not simply as black but as the embodiment of the afterlives of both slavery and colonialism: "'Look, a Negro!' It was a passing sting. I attempted a smile" (*Black Skin* 91). The tension between the sting and the attempted smile crystallizes an affective energy that reveals Fanon's "atmosphere of certain uncertainty" as the governing atmos-feeling. This racialized atmosphere, an interaction between body and air, rejects the overwhelming power of air that is always already out there, the "total climate" of anti-blackness, in Sharpe's formulation (104). The passing sting in response to being hailed as a "Negro" signals the black subject's affective response to the external, often violent stimulus of interpellation, while the attempted smile points to the "certain uncertainty" that marks not only the violence done to the black body but also the black subject's inward movement.

Kennedy returns to this atmosphere of "certain uncertainty" in the monologue *Sun* (1968), which she dedicated to Malcolm X. The character, identified only as Man, dies mid-performance while delivering the narrative of his life – similar to the monologue Othello delivers immediately before his suicide. *Sun* toggles between the Man's lyricism and the onstage violence he performs as he speaks. Kennedy seems to ask how he might hold on to his dreams in the midst of the violence that tears apart his body and leaves only the "[*v*]*anished Man's voice.*"[53] The monologue thus dramatizes the tension between the violence against black bodies and the freedom that cannot be understood if we imagine this violence as a totalizing force.

In *A Dying Colonialism* (1965), Fanon argues, "Under these conditions, the individual's breathing is an observed, an occupied breathing. It is a combat breathing" – constitutive of the atmos-feeling of black liberation.[54] In *Sun*, the intersection of the Man's lyricism with the violent forces that kill him – even as he steadfastly holds on to the lyrical – enacts Kennedy's interest in the combat breathing that can resist the occupied breathing produced by the afterlives of slavery and colonialism. Indeed, Man continues to speak after he dies, ending the play with the combat breathing of his final words: "I still" (61).

§

Just as Fanon's "combat breathing" cannot be separated from "occupied breathing," the twitch produced by the psychic hold of slavery coexists with the winks as writers loosen the psychic hold of slavery. The is-ness of African American literature continues to be profoundly shaped by the psychic hold of slavery and the psychic release from slavery.

Notes

1 Clifford Geertz, "Thick description: Toward an interpretive theory of culture" in *The Interpretation of Cultures* (New York: Basic Books, 1973), 3–30.
2 Stephen Best, *None like Us: Blackness, Belonging, Aesthetic Life* (Durham: Duke University Press, 2018)
3 Daniel Black, *The Coming* (New York: St. Martin's Press, 2015)
4 In *Beloved*, Morrison writes, "The picture is still there and what's more, if you go there--you who never was there–if you go there and stand in the place where it was, it will happen again; it will be there for you, waiting for you. So, Denver, you can't never go there. Never. Because even though it's all over– over and done with–it's going to always be there waiting for you."
5 Hortense Spillers, *Black, White, and in Color: Essays on American Literature and Culture* (Chicago: University of Chicago Press, 2003), 179.

Twitch or *Wink: The Literary* Afterlife of the Afterlife *of Slavery*

6   Toni Morrison, *A Mercy* (New York: Vintage Books, 2008), 179, 188.
7   Octavia Butler, *Kindred* (Boston: Beacon Press, 1979), 261.
8   Interview of Toni Morrison by Michel Martin. *NPR*. December 10, 2008.
9   Robert Stepto's *From Behind the Veil: A Study of Afro-American Narrative* (1979) is one of the first foundational texts that sets this linkage of writing and freedom in motion as the prime way of understanding the work of slave narratives.
10 Toni Morrison, *Beloved* (New York: Vintage, 2004), 164.
11 Morrison, *A Mercy*, 184.
12 Amiri Baraka (LeRoi Jones), *The Slave* in *Dutchman and the Slave* (New York: HarperCollins, 1964), 39-88. The language cited is on page 45.
13 Maya Lin, "Making the Memorial," *The New York Review of Books*, November 2, 2000.
14 Monifa Love, *Freedom in the Dismal* (Kaneohe, Hawaii: Plover Press, 1998), 13.
15 Edward P. Jones, *The Known World* (New York: Amistad, 2003), 84.
16 Ibid., 84.
17 Ibid., 138.
18 Malcolm X, "The Race Problem." African Students Association and NAACP Campus Chapter. Michigan State University, East Lansing, Michigan. 23 January 1963.
19 Jones, *Known World*, 341.
20 Jahan Ramazani, *The Hybrid Muse: Postcolonial Poetry in English* (Chicago: University of Chicago Press, 2001), 70.
21 This language was included in *Callaloo*'s 2015 call for papers for a special issue on Neo-Slave Narratives guest edited by Joan Anim-Addo (Goldsmiths, University of London) and Maria Helena Lima (SUNY Geneseo).
22 Colin Davis, "Hauntology, Spectres, and Phantoms," *French Studies* 59.3 (July 2005): 373–379.
23 In the introduction to *Black Skin, White Masks*, Frantz Fanon uses this word "epidermalization" as a more accurate description (more accurate than "internalization") of what happens when the "inferiority" of the blackened subject is written on the body.
24 Morrison, *A Mercy*, 194.

25 Stephen Best, "On Failing to Make the Past Present," *Modern Language Quarterly* 73.3 (September 2012): 472. (Best argues, "If *Beloved* incites melancholy, *A Mercy* incites mourning.")

26 The inspection is described in the following manner: "They point to a door that opens onto a stoneroom and there, standing among carriage boxes and a spinning wheel, they tell me to take off my clothes. Without touching they tell me what to do. To show them my teeth, my tongue. They frown at the candle burn on my palm, the one you kissed to cool. They look under my arms, between my legs. They circle me, lean down to inspect my feet. Naked under their examination I watch for what is in their eyes. No hate is there or scare or disgust but they are looking at me my body across distances without recognition. Swine look at me with more connection when they raise their heads from the trough. (Morrison, *A Mercy*, 133)

27 Frantz Fanon, *Black Skin, White Masks*, trans. Charles Markmann (New York: Grove Press, 1967), 109.

28 Morrison, *A Mercy*, 3.

29 Carolivia Herron, Thereafter Johnnie (New York: Vintage Books, 1991), 174.

30 Joy Leary, *Post Traumatic Slave Syndrome: America's Legacy of Enduring Injury and Healing* (Portand, Oregon: Uptone Press, 2005). The lecture I heard, in 2003, was delivered at the Albany Branch of the Hartford Public Library.

31 Ntozake Shange, "On 'What Is It We Really Harvestin' Here?" in *In Fact: The Best of Creative Nonfiction* (New York: Norton, 2005), 118.

32 Gwendolyn Brooks, *In The Mecca* (New York: Harper & Row, 1968), 54. In *Marxism and Literature*, Williams describes "structures of feeling" in the following manner: "It is a structured formation which, because it is at the very edge of semantic availability, has many characteristics of a pre-formation, until specific articulations – new semantic figures – are discovered in material practice: often, as it happens, in relatively isolated ways, which are only later seen to compose a significant (often in fact minority) generation: this often, in turn, the generation that substantially connects to its successor" (134). Raymond Williams, *Marxism and Literature* (Oxford: Oxford University Press, 1977), 134.

33 Amiri Baraka, *Slave Ship: A Historical Pageant. The Motion of History and Other Plays* (New York: Morrow, 1978), 132.

34 Paul Carter Harrison, *The Drama of Nommo* (New York: Grove, 1972), 35.
35 Ahmed, Sara. "Atmospheric Walls." *Feminist Killjoys*, 15 Sept. 2014, https://feministkilljoys.com/2014/09/15/atmospheric-walls.
36 Christina Sharpe, *In the Wake: On Blackness and Being* (Durham: Duke University Press, 2016), 102–34.
37 Stephen Best, *None like Us: Blackness, Belonging, Aesthetic Life* (Durham: Duke University Press, 2018), 21.
38 Hortense Spillers, "Changing the Letter: The Yokes, the Jokes of Discourse, or, Mrs. Stowe, Mr. Reed" in *Black, White, and in Color: Essays on American Literature and Culture* (Chicago: University of Chicago Press, 2003), 179.
39 Frantz Fanon, *Black Skins, White Masks*, trans. Richard Philcox (New York: Grove, 2008), 110.
40 Jared Sexton, "The Social Life of Social Death: On Afro-Pessimism and Black Optimism," *InTensions*, no. 5, 2011, 29, 22.
41 Amiri Baraka, *Slave Ship: A Historical Pageant. The Motion of History and Other Plays* (New York: Morrow, 1978), 132.
42 Toni Morrison, "The Slavebody and the Blackbody," *The Source of Self-Regard: Selected Essays, Speeches, and Meditations* (New York: Knopf, 2019), 74.
43 Amiri Baraka, *The Slave* in *Dutchman and The Slave* (New York: Perennial, 2001), 43.
44 The Roots. "Something in the Way of Things (In Town)." *Phrenology*, MCA, 2002.
45 A.B. Spellman, "Big Bushy Afros," *The International Review of African American Art*, vol. 15, no. 1, 1998, 53.
46 Ntozake Shange, *For Colored Girls Who Have Considered Suicide / When the Rainbow is Enuf* (New York: Scribner Poetry, 1997), xi.
47 Louis Althusser, "Ideology and Ideological State Apparatuses (Notes towards an Investigation)," *Lenin and Philosophy and Other Essays*, trans. Ben Brewster (New York: Monthly Review, 2001), 109.
48 Cheryl Clarke, *"After Mecca": Women Poets and the Black Arts Movement* (New Brunswick: Rutgers University Press, 2004), 120.
49 Ntozake Shange, *Sassafrass, Cypress and Indigo* (New York: St. Martin's, 2010), 22, 23, 31, 35, 39, 42.
50 "Ghoul." *Merriam-Webster Dictionary*, https://www.merriam-webster.com/dictionary/ghoul.

51 Adrienne Kennedy, "On the Writing of *Funnyhouse of a Negro*" in *The Adrienne Kennedy Reader* (Minneapolis: University of Minnesota Press, 2001), 27.
52 Frank B. Wilderson, *Red, White and Black: Cinema and the Structure of US Antagonisms* (Durham: Duke University Press, 2010), 52.
53 Adrienne Kennedy, *Sun* in *The Adrienne Kennedy Reader* (Minneapolis: University of Minnesota Press, 2001), 61.
54 Frantz Fanon, *A Dying Colonialism*, Trans. Haakon Chevalier (New York: Grove, 1965), 65.

CODA

> *As it grunts, twists, and pounds itself into being, it also dissipates, and its power startles and disappears simultaneously.*
> —Thomas DeFrantz, *Black Dance After Race*

In "Poets Who Are Negroes" (1950), Gwendolyn Brooks gives us the *is-ness* of African American literature when she muses, "Every negro poet has 'something to say.' His mere body, for that matter, is an eloquence. His quiet walk down the street is a speech to the people. *Is* a rebuke, *is* a plea, *is* a school" (italics mine). At the beginning of this aesthetic manifesto, Brooks foregrounds affect when she presents "that inspiriting emotion" that she likens to "tied hysteria." Just as Renee Gladman, in *Prose Architectures* (2017), shapes African American literature into line drawings that deliver the "density of knots" created through the "performance of doubt," Brooks' poetry created space within the production of African American literature for the ties that bind writers to the loose "school" of the "mere body."[1] Being bound to this flesh we might call a black body is complicated work. The tension of African American literature is the tension of nerve endings felt in the collective "quiet walk down the street" (as described by Brooks). When Hortense Spillers differentiates between oneness and individuality, she gives us the new grammar we need to understand the is-ness

---

What is African American Literature?, First Edition. Margo N. Crawford.
© 2021 John Wiley & Sons, Inc. Published 2021 by John Wiley & Sons, Inc.

of African American literature. What feels like a profoundly singular text that should not be grouped with others can also feel like it is a part of a profound tradition of singularity. Oneness is a way of refusing the logic of individuality necessarily set apart from a black collective.

The is-ness of African American literature is not fundamentally different from the is-ness of "incidental" identity and negotiated universalism that is beautifully rendered in the opening words of Bessie Head's *A Question of Power*. Head writes:

> It seemed almost incidental that he was African. So vast had inner perceptions grown over the years that he preferred an identification with mankind to an identification with a particular environment. And yet, as an African, he seemed to have made one of the most perfect statements: 'I am just anyone.'

I adore Head's emphasis on the fact that this character, Sello, makes this *perfect* statement of universalism as he is feeling "African." What makes "I am just anyone" such a perfect statement? The emphasis on "just" slides into the openness of "anyone" and makes us feel the stickiness of the open category, the traction to be felt in the unnaming, the way that the "just" makes "anyone" feel like it might be sufficient and foreclose any need for a more specific identification. The narrator, in the previous sentence, explains Sello's lack of the ability to identify with a "particular environment." When he speaks "as an African," he breaks out of his norm; his words "I am just anyone" emerge from the "particular environment" that makes him feel "African." Head shows how the environment of feeling differs from an environment of identity. Sello could not deliver the perfect statement "I am just anyone" if the words "as an African" signaled an environment of identity. The latter would produce the statement "I am just African." But, as an environment of feeling, the words "as an African," can signal that Sello feels shaped by the African-ness in a manner that is much more complicated than gaining the identity of an African. Head teaches us how to let go of the identity formation and lean into the environment of feeling embedded in the words "as an African."

CODA

In a similar sense, "as an African American," James Baldwin makes such a "perfect statement," in "Sonny's Blues" (arguably the most resonant short story in the tradition of African American literature), when he captures Sonny's tremendously hopeful present and his tremendously precarious future with the image of "the very cup of trembling." The affect explored in this book – the *blush*, the *vibration*, the *shiver* and *shock*, and the *twitch* or *wink*—lead us to African American literature as the "very cup of trembling." What *is* African American literature? On the lower frequencies, it is the trembling and not the cup. I end with a call to feel the density of the knots that fail to connect and "cup" Baldwin's trembling, Toni Morrison's blush ("Look where your hands are"), the poetics of vibration, the diasporic shock of elsewhere, and the twitch and wink produced by the psychic hold of slavery. Morrison ends *Beloved* with a description of rocking that creates tightness: "There is a loneliness that can be rocked. Arms crossed, knees drawn up; holding, holding on, this motion, unlike a ship's, smooths and contains the rocker. It's an inside kind—wrapped tight like skin" (274). Rocking that "contains" the rocker makes one feel embodied in disembodiment. The involuntary nature of a certain type of rocking happens when the body needs comfort or feels nervous. The comfort and the anxiety that shape the need to imagine the distinctiveness of the category "African American literature" is the comfort and anxiety of the rocking that produces the tightness that Morrison, at the end of *Beloved*, describes as "wrapped tight like skin."

African American literature is a wrapping and its tightest form is its loosest form – the affect that blushes, vibrates, shivers, twitches, and winks. African American literature shows that the form of affect is not an oxymoron. Affect is the form of formlessness in African American literature. In *The Forms of the Affects*, Eugenie Brinkema makes a powerful argument for "reading for affect" and approaching "affect as having form."[2] She argues that if we do not "read for affect as it inheres in form," we are only "documenting the stirrings of the skin" (37, 38). Reading African American literature for affect reveals that African American literature is more than

CODA

the documentation of the stirrings of the skin; the literary tradition is the stirring itself. The most-affect laden part of the final movement in *Beloved* is the statement "knuckles brushing a cheek in sleep seem to belong to the sleeper" (275). The knuckles and the brush of this tradition we can still call "African American literature" still seem to belong to we sleepers who feel the intimacy of the brushing of our cheeks as we keep reading.

Notes

1 John Vincler, "Dwelling Places, On Renee Gladman's Turn to Drawing," https://www.theparisreview.org/blog/2018/08/28/dwelling-places-on-renee-gladmans-turn-to-drawing/
2 Eugenie Brinkema, *The Forms of the Affects* (Durham: Duke University Press, 2014), 37–38.

Index

Adichie, Chimamanda, 104–106, 110, 131
African Treasury, An, 116
Afro-American Literature: The Reconstruction of Instruction, 5, 23
Ahmed, Sara, 26, 152–153, 167, 173
Aidoo, Ama Ata, 107–110, 131
Americanah, 104–106, 110, 131
Ask Your Mama, 55–72

Bakhtin, Michael, 34
Baldwin, James, 177
Baraka, Amiri, 6, 7, 14, 15, 16, 17, 21, 23, 24–25, 39–40, 46, 48, 55–56, 61–72, 104–105, 118–119, 122–125, 129–133
Beloved, 20, 24, 35, 38, 49–50, 136, 139, 141, 149–150, 170–172
Berlant, Lauren, 7, 29, 52
Best, Stephen, 33, 52, 135

Black Arts Movement, 5, 9, 13, 14, 15, 19, 46, 50–51, 151–152, 154–158, 160–162, 165–166, 173
Black Book, The, 10, 11, 13, 14, 15, 19, 20, 24
Black Boy, 118
Black Misery, 69–72
Black Skin, White Masks, 136, 167, 172
Black, Daniel, 135
Blake, Felice, 9
Bluest Eye, The, 32, 35–38, 42–44, 50–51
Blues People, 152, 154
Bontemps, Arna, 115–116, 131
Brand, Dionne, 9, 111
Brennan, Teresa, 39
Brinkema, Eugenie, 177
Brooks, Gwendolyn, 4, 23, 103, 119–124, 128, 132–133, 175
Butler, Octavia, 25, 137, 171

What is African American Literature?, First Edition. Margo N. Crawford.
© 2021 John Wiley & Sons, Inc. Published 2021 by John Wiley & Sons, Inc.

Index

Cane, 8, 23, 85–96, 98, 100
Carlson-Wee, Anders, 26, 27
Citizen, 10, 11, 29
Clifton, Lucille, 112, 131
Colbert, Stephen, 1
Coming, The, 135–136, 170
Corregidora, 25
Cortez, Jayne, 29
Crawley, Ashon T., 7, 23

Danticat, Edwidge, 104, 130
DeCarava, Roy, 29
DeFrantz, Thomas, 175
Douglass, Frederick, 27, 28, 52
Drama of Nommo, The, 152, 173

Ellison, Ralph, 4, 5, 11, 23
Equiano, Olaudah, 31
Erasure, 10, 11, 12, 13
Everett, Percival, 10, 11, 12, 13

Fanon, Frantz, 34, 35, 36, 45, 52, 136, 149–150, 154, 167–174
Flatley, Jonathan, 22, 24, 103
Forms of the Affects, The, 177
Freedom in the Dismal, 138, 142, 144, 171
Funnyhouse of a Negro, 155, 165, 167–168, 174

Gates, Henry Louis, 6, 14, 15
Geertz, Clifford, 135
Genette, Gérard, 9, 13
Giddings, Paula, 82, 84
Gillespie, Michael, 6, 23, 60, 72
Giovanni, Nikki, 80–84, 99
Gladman, Renee, 175

Glissant, Edouard, 103–106, 109, 111, 113–114, 130, 134
God Help the Child, 20, 32, 35–51
Griffin, Farah Jasmine, 44
Grosvenor, Vertamae, 76–77, 99
Gumbs, Alexis Pauline, 6, 7, 23, 75, 99

Head, Bessie, 113–115, 117, 124, 129, 131, 176
Henderson, Stephen, 73, 74, 99
Holiday, Billie, 39–43, 52
Hughes, Langston, 29, 55–60, 62–72, 113–116, 131
Hurston, Zora Neale, 26, 103, 130

In Our Terribleness, 14, 15, 17, 18, 24, 55–57, 61–63, 65–71
Interesting Narrative of the Life of Olaudah Equiano, The, 31

Jacobs, Harriet, 3, 22
Jameson, Fredric, 22, 24, 28, 42
Jazz, 29, 31, 34, 37, 42, 52
Jefferson, Thomas, 28
Jones, Gayl, 25

Keene, John, 96–98, 101
Kennedy, Adrienne, 155, 165–170, 174
Kgositsile, Keorapetse, 117–134
Kindred, 137, 171
Known World, The, 138, 144–146, 151, 171

Lacan, Jacques, 50
Locke, Alain, 2, 3, 22

180

Index

Ligon, Glenn, 10, 11
Lin, Maya, 141, 171
Lorde, Audre, 25, 36, 45
Love, Monifa, 138, 142–143, 171

Malamud, Bernard, 18, 19
Map to the Door of No Return, A, 111
Merleau-Ponty, Maurice, 63
Mercy, A, 38, 42, 137–141, 148–151, 171–172
Michaels, Walter Benn, 3, 23
Morrison, Toni, 1, 2, 14, 15, 20, 24, 25, 26, 29, 31, 32, 33, 34, 35, 36, 37, 38, 39–53, 177
Moten Fred, 2, 4, 8, 22, 73, 77, 83, 99
Muñoz, José Esteban, 153

Native Son, 11, 12, 13, 118
Neal, Larry, 73, 84, 100
New Negro Movement, 2, 3, 5, 22
None Like Us, 135–136, 153, 155, 170, 173
North, Michael, 5

Our Sister Killjoy, 107–108, 131

Paradise, 32–35
paratexts, 9, 11, 13, 16, 29, 43
Phillips, Rowan Ricardo, 79, 99
Physics of Blackness, The, 111
Poetics of Relation, 103, 130, 134
Poetry of the Negro, The, 115
post-neo-slave narratives, 137–139, 141, 144
Puryear, Martin, 87–89, 96, 100

Question of Power, A, 176

Randall, Dudley, 13
Rankine, Claudia, 10, 11, 29, 52
Ringgold, Faith, 50
Rushdy, Ashraf, 138

Seismosis, 96–98, 101
Selasi, Taiye, 104, 106, 131
Sexton, Jared, 154, 156, 173
Shange, Ntozake, 151, 155, 162–165, 172–173
shiver, 103–115, 117, 128, 130
Shouse, Eric, 31
Signifying Monkey, The, 6
Slave, The, 138–139, 156, 159–161, 171, 173
Slave Ship, 152, 154, 156–160, 172–173
Smith, Tracy, 10
"Sonny's Blues," 177
Spillers, Hortense, 136, 153, 155, 161, 165, 170, 173, 175
Stackhouse, Christopher, 96–98, 101
Stepto, Robert, 5, 23
Surface reading, 33
Sweet Flypaper of Life, The, 29

Tar Baby, 32, 47
Tenants, The, 18, 19
Toomer, Jean, 8, 23, 85–96, 98, 100, 101

Vincler, John, 178

Index

Walker, Alice, 77–78, 80–81, 90, 93, 99
Walker, Kara, 38, 40, 44–46, 51
Walker, Margaret, 80, 99
Wall, Cheryl, 9
Warren, Kenneth, 21
What Was African American Literature?, 21

Wheatley, Phillis, 28, 75–80, 83–85, 99
Worrying the Line, 9
Wright, Michelle, 111
Wright, Richard, 11, 24

Young, Kevin, 84, 100